LUKE, PETER, BARNABAS, SILAS, AND TIMOTHY TELL THEIR STORY

THE

BOOK OF ACTS

IN

FIRST PERSON

LUKE, PETER, BARNABAS,
SILAS, AND TIMOTHY
TELL THEIR STORY

THE

BOOK OF ACTS

IN

FIRST PERSON

Luke, Peter, Barnabas,Silas, and Timothy Tell Their Story

The Book of Acts
In First Person

Copyright
MM
Published by
SEEDSOWERS
Publishing House

Based on the *Holy Bible*, New Living Translation, copyright©
1996. Used by permission of Tyndale House Publishers, Inc.,
Wheaton, Illinois 60189. All rights reserved.

Printed in
the United States of America

Published by
SEEDSOWERS
Christian Books Publishing House
P.O. Box3317
Jacksonville, FL 32206
(800) 228-2665
www.seedsowers.com

Library of Congress Cataloging-In-Publication Data

ISBN 0-940232-78-2
1. Religious
2. Non-Fiction

LUKE
PRESENTS
THE PROLOGUE
TO ACTS

PROLOGUE

In my first book, Theophilus, I told you about everything Jesus began to do and teach until the day he ascended to heaven after giving his chosen apostles further instructions from the Holy Spirit. During the forty days after his crucifixion, he appeared to the apostles from time to time and proved to them in many ways that he was actually alive. On these occasions he talked to them about the Kingdom of God.

In one of these meetings as he was eating a meal with them, he told them, "Do not leave Jerusalem until the Father sends you what he promised. Remember, I have told you about this before. John baptized with water, but in just a few days you will be baptized with the Holy Spirit."

When the apostles were with Jesus, they kept asking him, "Lord, are you going to free Israel now and restore our kingdom?"

"The Father sets those dates," he replied, "and they are not for you to know. But when the Holy Spirit has come upon you, you will receive power and will tell people about me everywhere—in Jerusalem, throughout Judea, in Samaria, and to the ends of the earth."

Bethany

It was not long after he said this that Jesus was taken up into the sky while they were watching, and he disappeared into a cloud. As they were straining their eyes to see him, two white-robed men suddenly stood there among them. They said, "Men of Galilee, why are you standing here staring at the sky? Jesus has been taken away from you into heaven. And someday, just as you saw him go, he will return!"

Luke, AD 63

Acts 1:1-11

1

PETER

BEGINS THE STORY

AD 30-41

Acts 1:12-11:24

After the Ascension

We apostles were at the Mount of Olives when the Lord ascended, so we walked the half mile back to Jerusalem. Then we went to the upstairs room of the house where we were staying. Here is the list of those of us who were present, including me (Peter):

> John,
> James,
> Andrew,
> Philip,
> Thomas,
> Bartholomew,
> Matthew,
> James (son of Alphaeus),
> Simon (the Zealot),
> and Judas (son of James).

We all met together continually for prayer, along with Mary the mother of Jesus, several other women, and the brothers of Jesus.

During this time, on a day when about 120 believers were present, I stood up and addressed them as follows:

"Brothers and sisters, it was necessary for the Scriptures to be fulfilled concerning Judas, who guided the temple police to arrest Jesus. This was predicted long ago by the Holy Spirit, speaking through King David. Judas was one of us, chosen to share in the ministry with us."

(Judas bought a field with the money he received for his treachery, and falling there, he burst open, spilling out his intestines. The news of his death spread rapidly among all the people of Jerusalem, and they gave the place the Aramaic name Akeldama, which means Field of Blood.)

I continued, "This was predicted in the book of Psalms, where it says,

> *Let his home become desolate, with no one living in it.*

Ps. 69:25

5

And again,

Let his position be given to someone else.

Ps. 109:8

"So now we must choose another man to take Judas's place. It must be someone who has been with us all the time that we were with the Lord Jesus—from the time he was baptized by John until the day he was taken from us into heaven. Whoever is chosen will join us as a witness of Jesus' resurrection."

So we nominated two men: Joseph called Barsabbas (also known as Justus) and Matthias. Then we all prayed for the right man to be chosen. "O Lord," we said, "you know every heart. Show us which of these men you have chosen as an apostle to replace Judas the traitor in this ministry, for he has deserted us and gone where he belongs." Then we cast lots, and in this way Matthias was chosen and became an apostle with us eleven.

The Day of Pentecost

Spring, AD 30   Chapter 2

On the day of Pentecost, seven weeks after Jesus' resurrection, we believers were meeting together in one place. Suddenly, there was a sound from heaven like the roaring of a mighty windstorm in the skies above us, and it filled the house where we were meeting. Then, what looked like flames or tongues of fire appeared and settled on each of us. And everyone present was filled with the Holy Spirit and began to speak in other tongues, as the Holy Spirit gave us this ability.

Godly Jews from many nations were living in Jerusalem at this time. When they heard this sound, they came running to see what it was all about, and they were bewildered to hear their own languages being spoken by us. They were beside themselves with wonder.

"How can this be?" they exclaimed. "These people are from Galilee, and yet we hear them speaking the languages of the lands where we were born! Here we are—Parthians, Medes, Elamites, people from Mesopotamia, Judea, Cappadocia, Pontus, the province of Asia, Phrygia, Pamphylia, Egypt, and the areas of Libya toward Cyrene, visitors from Rome (both Jews and converts to Judaism), Cretans, and Arabians. And we all hear these people speaking in our own languages about the wonderful things God has done!" They stood there amazed and perplexed. "What can this mean?" they asked each other.

But others in the crowd were mocking. "They are drunk, that's all!" they said.

Then I stepped forward with the eleven other apostles and shouted to the crowd, "Listen carefully, all of you, fellow Jews and residents of Jerusalem! Make no mistake about this. Some of you are saying these people are drunk. It is not true! It is much too early for that. People do not get drunk by nine o'clock in the morning. No, what you see this morning was predicted centuries ago by the prophet Joel:

> *In the last days, God said, 'I will pour out my Spirit upon all people. Your sons and your daughters will prophesy, your young men will see visions, and your old men will dream dreams. In those days I will pour out my Spirit upon all my servants, men and women alike, and they will prophesy. And I will cause wonders in the heavens above and signs on the earth below—blood and fire and clouds of smoke. The sun will be turned into darkness, and the moon will turn blood-red, before that great and glorious day of the Lord arrives. And anyone who calls on the name of the Lord will be saved.'*

Joel 2:28-32

"People of Israel, listen! God publicly endorsed Jesus of Nazareth by doing wonderful miracles, wonders, and signs through him, as you well know. But you followed God's prearranged plan. With the help of lawless Gentiles, you

7

nailed him to the cross and murdered him. However, God released him from the horrors of death and raised him back to life again, for death could not keep him in its grip. King David said this about him:

> *I know the Lord is always with me, I will not be shaken, for he is right beside me. No wonder my heart is filled with joy and my mouth shouts his praises! My body rests in hope. For you will not leave my soul among the dead or allow your Holy One to rot in the grave. You have shown me the way of life, and you will give me wonderful joy in your presence.*
>
> Ps. 16:8-11

"Dear brothers and sisters, think about this! David was not referring to himself when he spoke these words I have quoted, for he died and was buried, and his tomb is still here among us. But he was a prophet, and he knew God had promised with an oath that one of David's own descendants would sit on David's throne as the Messiah. David was looking into the future and predicting the Messiah's resurrection. He was saying that the Messiah would not be left among the dead and that his body would not rot in the grave.

"This prophecy was speaking of Jesus, whom God raised from the dead, and we all are witnesses of this. Now he sits on the throne of highest honor in heaven, at God's right hand. And the Father, as he had promised, gave him the Holy Spirit to pour out upon us, just as you see and hear today. For David himself never ascended into heaven, yet he said,

> *The LORD said to my Lord, 'Sit in honor at my right hand until I humble your enemies, making them a footstool under your feet.'*
>
> Ps. 110:1

8

"So let it be clearly known by everyone in Israel that God has made this Jesus whom you crucified to be both Lord and Messiah!"

My words convicted them deeply, and they said to me and to the other apostles, "Brothers, what should we do?"

I replied, "Each of you must turn from your sins and turn to God and be baptized in the name of Jesus Christ for the forgiveness of your sins. Then you will receive the gift of the Holy Spirit. This promise is to you and to your children, and even to the Gentiles—all who have been called by the Lord our God."

Then I continued preaching for a long time, strongly urging all my listeners, "Save yourselves from this generation that has gone astray!"

Those who believed what I said were baptized and added to the church—about three thousand in all. They joined with the other believers and devoted themselves to the apostles' teaching and fellowship, sharing in the Lord's Supper and prayer.

A deep sense of awe came over them all, and we apostles performed many miraculous signs and wonders.

AD 30-31

And all of us believers met together constantly and shared everything we had. We sold our possessions and shared the proceeds with those in need. We worshiped together at the Temple each day, met in homes for the Lord's Supper, and shared our meals with great joy and generosity—all the while praising God and enjoying the goodwill of all the people. And each day the Lord added to our group those who were being saved.

I, Peter, Healed a Lame Man

Chapter 3

John and I went to the Temple one afternoon to take part in the three o'clock prayer service. As we approached the Temple, a man lame from birth was being carried in. Each day he was put beside the Temple gate, the one called the Beautiful Gate, so he could beg from the people going into the Temple. When he saw John and me about to enter, he asked us for some money. John and I looked at him intently, and I said, "Look at us!" The lame man looked at us eagerly, expecting a gift. But I said, "I do not have any money for you. But I will give you what I have. In the name of Jesus Christ of Nazareth, get up and walk!"

Then I took the lame man by the right hand and helped him up. And as I did, the man's feet and anklebones were healed and strengthened. He jumped up, stood on his feet, and began to walk! Then, walking, leaping, and praising God, he went into the Temple with us.

All the people saw him walking and heard him praising God. When they realized he was the lame beggar they had seen so often at the Beautiful Gate, they were absolutely astounded! They all rushed out to Solomon's Colonnade, where he was holding tightly to John and me. Everyone stood there in awe of the wonderful thing that had happened.

I saw my opportunity and addressed the crowd. "People of Israel," I said, "what is so astounding about this? And why look at us as though we had made this man walk by our own power and godliness? For it is the God of Abraham, the God of Isaac, the God of Jacob, the God of all our ancestors who brought glory to his servant Jesus by doing this. This is the same Jesus whom you handed over and rejected before Pilate, despite Pilate's decision to release him. You rejected this holy, righteous one and instead demanded the release of a murderer. You killed the author of life, but God raised him to life. And we are witnesses of this fact!

"The name of Jesus has healed this man—and you know how lame he was before. Faith in Jesus' name has caused this healing before your very eyes.

"Friends, I realize that what you did to Jesus was done in ignorance; and the same can be said of your leaders. But God was fulfilling what all the prophets had declared about the Messiah beforehand—that he must suffer all these things. Now turn from your sins and turn to God, so you can be cleansed of your sins. Then wonderful times of refreshment will come from the presence of the Lord, and he will send

Jesus your Messiah to you again. For he must remain in heaven until the time for the final restoration of all things, as God promised long ago through his prophets. Moses said,

> *The Lord your God will raise up a Prophet like me from among your own people. Listen carefully to everything he tells you.*
>
> Deut. 18:15

Then Moses said,

> *Anyone who will not listen to that Prophet will be cut off from God's people and utterly destroyed.*
>
> Deut. 18:19

"Starting with Samuel, every prophet spoke about what is happening today. You are the children of those prophets, and you are included in the covenant God promised your ancestors. For God said to Abaraham,

> *Through your descendants all the families on earth will be blessed.*
>
> Gen. 22:18; 26:4

"When God raised up his servant, he sent him first to you people of Israel, to bless you by turning each of you back from your sinful ways."

John and I Are Arrested

AD 31   Chapter 4

While John and I were speaking to the people, the leading priests, the captain of the temple guard, and some of the Sadducees came over to us. They were very disturbed that John and I were claiming, on the authority of Jesus, that there was a resurrection of the dead. They arrested us and, since it was already evening, jailed us until morning. But many people who heard our message believed it, so that the number of believers totaled about five thousand men, not counting women and children.

The next day the council of all the rulers and elders and teachers of religious law met in Jerusalem. Annas the high priest was there, along with Caiaphas, John, Alexander, and other relatives of the high priest. They brought the two of us in and demanded, "By what power, or in whose name, have you done this?"

Then, filled with the Holy Spirit, I said to them, "Leaders and elders of our nation, are we being questioned because we have done a good deed for a crippled man? Do you want to know how he was healed? Let me clearly state to you and to all the people of Israel that he was healed in the name and power of Jesus Christ from Nazareth, the man you crucified, but whom God raised from the dead. For Jesus is the one referred to in the Scriptures, where it says,

The stone that you builders rejected has now become the cornerstone.

Ps.118:22

There is salvation in no one else! There is no other name in all of heaven for people to call on to save them."

The members of the council were amazed when they saw the boldness of John and me, for they could see that we were ordinary men who had had no special training. They also recognized us as men who had been with Jesus. But since the man who had been healed was standing right there among us, the council had nothing to say. So they sent John and me out of the council chamber and conferred among themselves.

"What should we do with these men?" they asked each other. "We cannot deny they have done a miraculous sign, and everybody in Jerusalem knows about it. But perhaps we can stop them from spreading their propaganda. We will warn them not to speak to anyone in Jesus' name again. So they called us back in and told us never again to speak or teach about Jesus."

But John and I replied, "Do you think God wants us to obey you rather than him? We cannot stop telling about the wonderful things we have seen and heard."

The council then threatened us further, but they finally let us go because they did not know how to punish us without starting a riot. For everyone was praising God for this miraculous sign—the healing of a man who had been lame for more than forty years.

As soon as we were freed, John and I found the believers and told them what the leading priests and elders had said. Then all the believers were united as we lifted our voices in prayer: "O Sovereign Lord, Creator of heaven and earth, the sea, and everything in them–you spoke long ago by the Holy Spirit through our ancestor King David, your servant, saying,

> *Why did the nations rage? Why did the*
> *people waste their time with futile plans?*
> *The kings of earth prepared for battle; the*
> *rulers gathered together against the Lord*
> *and against his Messiah.*

Ps. 2:1-2

"That is what has happened here in this city! For Herod Antipas, Pontius Pilate the governor, the Gentiles, and the people of Israel were all united against Jesus, your holy servant, whom you anointed. In fact, everything they did occurred according to your eternal will and plan. And now, O Lord, hear their threats, and give your servants great boldness in their preaching. Send your healing power; may miraculous signs and wonders be done through the name of your holy servant Jesus."

After this prayer, the building where we were meeting shook, and we were all filled with the Holy Spirit. And we preached God's message with boldness.

All the believers were of one heart and one mind, and we felt that what we owned was not our own; we shared everything we had. And we apostles gave powerful witness to the resurrection of the Lord Jesus, and God's great favor was upon us all. There was no poverty among us, because people who owned land or houses sold them and brought the money to those of us who were apostles for those in need.

Ananias and Sapphira Die at My Feet

AD 32

There was also a man named Ananias who, with his wife Sapphira, sold some property. He brought part of the money to us apostles, but he claimed it was the full amount. His wife agreed to this deception.

Then I said, "Ananias, why has Satan filled your heart? You lied to the Holy Spirit, and you kept some of the money for yourself. The property was yours to sell or not sell, as you wished. And after selling it, the money was yours to give away. How could you do a thing like this? You were not lying to us but to God."

As soon as Ananias heard these words, he fell to the floor and died. Everyone who heard about it was terrified. Then some young men wrapped him in a sheet and took him out and buried him.

About three hours later his wife came in, not knowing what had happened. I asked her, "Was this the price you and your husband received for your land?"

"Yes," she replied, "that was the price."

And I said, "How could the two of you even think of doing a thing like this—conspiring together to test the Spirit of the Lord? Just outside that door are the young men who buried your husband, and they will carry you out, too."

Instantly, she fell to the floor and died. When the young men came in and saw that she was dead, they carried her out and buried her beside her husband. Great fear gripped the entire church and all others who heard what had happened.

All Twelve of Us Are Imprisoned

Meanwhile, we apostles were performing many miraculous signs and wonders among the people. And the believers were meeting regularly at the Temple in the area known as

Solomon's Colonnade. No one else dared to join us, though everyone had high regard for us. And more and more people believed and were brought to the Lord—crowds of both men and women. As a result of our work, sick people were brought out into the streets on beds and mats so that my shadow might fall across some of them as I went by. Crowds came in from the villages around Jerusalem, bringing their sick and those possessed by evil spirits, and they were all healed.

The high priest and his friends, who were Sadducees, reacted with violent jealousy. They arrested us apostles and put us in jail. But an angel of the Lord came in the night, opened the gates of the jail, and brought us out. Then he told us, "Go to the Temple and give the people this message of life!" So we entered the Temple about daybreak and immediately began teaching.

When the high priest and his officials arrived, they convened the high council, along with all the elders of Israel. Then they sent for us to be brought for trial. But when the Temple guards went to the jail, we were gone. So they returned to the council and reported, "The jail was locked, with the guards standing outside, but when we opened the gates, no one was there!"

When the captain of the Temple guard and the leading priests heard this, they were perplexed, wondering where it would all end. Then someone arrived with the news that the men they had jailed were out in the Temple, teaching the people.

The captain went with his Temple guards and arrested us, but without violence, for they were afraid the people would kill them if they treated us roughly. Then they brought us apostles in before the council. "Did we not tell you never again to teach in this man's name?" the high priest demanded. "Instead, you have filled all Jerusalem with your teaching about Jesus, and you intend to blame us for his death!"

But the other apostles and I replied, "We must obey God rather than human authority. The God of our ancestors raised Jesus from the dead after you killed him by crucifying him. Then God put him in the place of honor at his right hand as Prince and Savior. He did this to give the people of

Israel an opportunity to turn from their sins and turn to God so their sins would be forgiven. We are witnesses of these things and so is the Holy Spirit, who is given by God to those who obey him."

At this, the high council was furious and decided to kill us. But one member had a different perspective. He was a Pharisee named Gamaliel, who was an expert on religious law and was very popular with the people. He stood up and ordered that we be sent outside the council chamber for a while. Then he addressed his colleagues as follows: "Men of Israel, take care what you are planning to do to these men! Some time ago there was that fellow Theudas, who pretended to be someone great. About four hundred others joined him, but he was killed, and his followers went their various ways. The whole movement came to nothing. After him, at the time of the census, there was Judas of Galilee. He got some people to follow him, but he was killed, too, and all his followers scattered.

"So my advice is, leave these men alone. If they are teaching and doing these things merely on their own, it will soon be overthrown. But if it is of God, you will not be able to stop them. You may even find yourselves fighting against God."

The council accepted his advice. They called us in and had us flogged. Then they ordered us never again to speak in the name of Jesus, and they let us go. We left the high council rejoicing that God had counted us worthy to suffer dishonor for the name of Jesus. And every day, in the Temple and in our homes, we continued to teach and preach this message: "The Messiah you are looking for is Jesus."

We Appointed Seven Men

AD 33

Chapter 6:1-7

But as the believers rapidly multiplied, there were rumblings of discontent. Those who spoke Greek complained against those who spoke Hebrew, saying that their widows were being discriminated against in the daily distribution of food. So we twelve called a meeting of all the believers.

"We apostles should spend our time preaching and teaching the word of God, not administering a food program," we said. "Now look around among yourselves, brothers and sisters, and select seven men who are well respected and are full of the Holy Spirit and wisdom. We will put them in charge of this business. Then we can spend our time in prayer and preaching and teaching the word."

This idea pleased the whole group, and they chose the following: Stephen (a man full of faith and the Holy Spirit), Philip, Procorus, Nicanor, Timon, Parmenas, and Nicolas of Antioch (a Gentile convert to the Jewish faith, who had now become a Christian). These seven were presented to us apostles, and we prayed for them as we laid our hands on them.

God's message was preached in ever-widening circles. The number of believers increased in Jerusalem, and many of the Jewish priests were converted, too.

Stephen Is Arrested

AD 36   Chapter 6:8-15

Stephen, a man full of God's grace and power, performed amazing miracles and signs among the people. But one day some men from the Synagogue of Freed Slaves, as it was called, started a debate with him. They were Jews from Cyrene, Alexandria, Cilicia, and the province of Asia. None of them was able to stand against the wisdom and Spirit by which Stephen spoke.

So they persuaded some men to lie about Stephen, saying, "We heard him blaspheme Moses, and even God." Naturally, this roused the crowds, the elders, and the teachers of religious law. So they arrested Stephen and brought him before the high council. The lying witnesses said, "This man is always speaking against the Temple and against the law of Moses. We have heard him say that this Jesus of Nazareth will destroy the Temple and change the customs Moses handed down to us." At this point everyone in the council stared at Stephen because his face became as bright as an angel's.

Stephen Was Stoned

Chapter 7

Then the high priest asked Stephen, "Are these accusations true?"

This was Stephen's reply: "Brothers and honorable fathers, listen to me. Our glorious God appeared to our ancestor Abraham in Mesopotamia before he moved to Haran. God told him,

> *Leave your native land and your relatives,*
> *and come to the land that I will show you.*
>
> Gen. 12:1

"So Abraham left the land of the Chaldeans and lived in Haran until his father died. Then God brought him here to the land where you now live. But God gave him no inheritance here, not even one square foot of land. God did promise, however, that eventually the whole country would belong to Abraham and his descendants—though he had no children yet. But God also told him,

> *Your descendants will live in a foreign*
> *country where they will be mistreated as*
> *slaves for four hundred years. But I will*
> *punish the nation that enslaves them, and in*
> *the end they will come out and worship me*
> *in this place.*
>
> Gen. 15:13-14; Ex. 3:12b

"God also gave Abraham the covenant of circumcision at that time. And so Isaac, Abraham's son, was circumcised when he was eight days old. Isaac became the father of Jacob, and Jacob was the father of the twelve patriarchs of the Jewish nation.

"These sons of Jacob were very jealous of their brother Joseph, and they sold him to be a slave in Egypt. But God was with him and delivered him from his anguish. And God gave him favor before Pharaoh, king of Egypt. God also gave Joseph unusual wisdom, so that Pharaoh appointed him governor over all of Egypt and put him in charge of all the affairs of the palace.

"But a famine came upon Egypt and Canaan. There was great misery for our ancestors, as they ran out of food. Jacob heard that there was still grain in Egypt, so he sent his sons to buy some. The second time they went, Joseph revealed his identity to his brothers, and they were introduced to Pharaoh. Then Joseph sent for his father, Jacob, and all his relatives to come to Egypt, seventy-five persons in all. So Jacob went to Egypt. He died there, as did all his sons. All of them were taken to Shechem and buried in the tomb Abraham had bought from the sons of Hamor in Shechem.

"As the time drew near when God would fulfill his promise to Abraham, the number of our people in Egypt greatly increased. But then a new king came to the throne of Egypt who knew nothing about Joseph. This king plotted against our people and forced parents to abandon their newborn babies so they would die.

"At that time Moses was born—a beautiful child in God's eyes. His parents cared for him at home for three months. When at last they had to abandon him, Pharaoh's daughter found him and raised him as her own son. Moses was taught all the wisdom of the Egyptians, and he became mighty in both speech and action.

"One day when he was forty years old, he decided to visit his relatives, the people of Israel. During this visit, he saw an Egyptian mistreating a man of Israel. So Moses came to his defense and avenged him, killing the Egyptian. Moses assumed his brothers would realize that God had sent him to rescue them, but they did not.

"The next day he visited them again and saw two men of Israel fighting. He tried to be a peacemaker. 'Men,' he said, 'you are brothers. Why are you hurting each other?'

"But the man in the wrong pushed Moses aside and told him to mind his own business. 'Who made you a ruler and judge over us?' he asked. 'Are you going to kill me as you killed the Egyptian yesterday?' When Moses heard that, he fled the country and lived as a foreigner in the land of Midian, where his two sons were born.

"Forty years later, in the desert near Mount Sinai, an angel appeared to Moses in the flame of a burning bush. Moses saw it and wondered what it was. As he went to see, the voice of the Lord called out to him,

> *I am the God of your ancestors—the God of Abraham, Isaac, and Jacob.*
>
> Exodus 3:6

Moses shook with terror and dared not to look. And the Lord said to him,

> *Take off your sandals, for you are standing on holy ground. You can be sure that I have seen the misery of my people in Egypt. I have heard their cries. So I have to rescue them. Now go, for I will send you to Egypt.*
>
> Exodus 3:5, 7-10

"And so God sent back the same man his people had previously rejected by demanding, 'Who made you ruler and judge over us?' Through the angel who appeared to him in the burning bush, Moses was sent to be their ruler and savior. And by means of many miraculous signs and wonders, he led them out of Egypt, through the Red Sea, and back and forth through the wilderness for forty years.

"Moses himself told the people of Israel,

> *God will raise up a Prophet like me from among your own people.*
>
> Deut. 18:15

"Moses was with the assembly of God's people in the wilderness. He was the mediator between the people of Israel and the angel who gave him life-giving words on Mount Sinai to pass on to us.

"But our ancestors rejected Moses and wanted to return to Egypt. They told Aaron, 'Make us some gods who can lead us, for we do not know what has become of this Moses, who brought us out of Egypt.' So they made an idol shaped like a calf, and they sacrificed to it and rejoiced in this thing they had made. Then God turned away from them and gave them up to serve the sun, moon, and stars as their gods! In the book of the prophets it is written,

> *Was it to me you were bringing sacrifices during those forty years in the wilderness, Israel? No, your real interest was in your pagan gods—the shrine of Molech, the star god Rephan, and the images you made to worship them. So I will send you into captivity far away in Babylon.*
>
> Amos 5:25-27

"Our ancestors carried the Tabernacle with them through the wilderness. It was constructed in exact accordance with the plan shown to Moses by God. Years later, when Joshua led the battles against the Gentile nations that God drove out of this land, the Tabernacle was taken with them into their new territory. And it was used there until the time of King David.

"David found favor with God and asked for the privilege of building a permanent Temple for the God of Jacob. But it was Solomon who actually built it. However, the Most High does not live in temples made by human hands. As the prophet says,

> *'Heaven is my home, and the earth is my footstool. Could you ever build me a temple as good as that?' asks the Lord. 'Could you build a dwelling place for me? Did I not make everything in heaven and earth?*
>
> Is. 66:1-2

"You stubborn people! You are heathen at heart and deaf to the truth. Must you forever resist the Holy Spirit? But your ancestors did, and so do you! Name one prophet your ancestors did not persecute! They even killed the ones who predicted the coming of the Righteous One—the Messiah whom you betrayed and murdered. You deliberately disobeyed God's law, although you received it from the hands of angels."

The Jewish leaders were infuriated by Stephen's accusation, and they shook their fists in rage. But Stephen, full of the Holy Spirit, gazed steadily upward into heaven and saw the glory of God, and he saw Jesus standing in the place of honor at God's right hand. And he told them, "Look, I see the heavens opened and the Son of Man standing in the place of honor at God's right hand!"

Then they put their hands over their ears, and drowning out his voice with their shouts, they rushed at him. They dragged him out of the city and began to stone him. The official witnesses took off their coats and laid them at the feet of a young man named Saul.

And as they stoned him, Stephen prayed, "Lord Jesus, receive my spirit." And he fell to his knees, shouting, "Lord, do not charge them with this sin!" And with that, he died.

Saul Persecuted Us

AD 37   Chapter 8:1-3

Saul was one of the official witnesses at the killing of Stephen. A great wave of persecution began that day, sweeping over the church in Jerusalem; and all the believers except us apostles fled into Judea and Samaria. (Some godly men came and buried Stephen with loud weeping.) Saul was going everywhere to devastate the church. He went from house to house, dragging out both men and women to throw them in jail.

But the believers who had fled Jerusalem went everywhere preaching the Good News about Jesus.

Philip Proclaims Christ

Chapter 8:4-13

Philip, for example, went to the city of Samaria and told people there about the Messiah. Crowds listened intently to what he had to say because of the miracles he did. Many evil spirits were cast out, screaming as they left their victims.

And many who had been paralyzed or lame were healed. So there was great joy in that city.

A man named Simon had been a sorcerer there for many years, claiming to be someone great. The Samaritan people, from the least to the greatest, often spoke of him as "the Great One—the Power of God." He was very influential because of the magic he performed. But now the people believed Philip's message of Good News concerning the Kingdom of God and the name of Jesus Christ. As a result, many men and women were baptized. Then Simon himself believed and was baptized. He began following Philip wherever he went, and he was amazed by the great miracles and signs Philip performed.

John and I Traveled to Samaria

Samaria, AD 37   Chapter 8:14-25

When we apostles back in Jerusalem heard that the people of Samaria had accepted God's message, we decided that John and I should go there. As soon as we arrived, we prayed for these new Christians to receive the Holy Spirit. The Holy Spirit had not yet come upon any of them, for they had not been baptized in the name of the Lord Jesus. Then John and I laid our hands upon these believers, and they received the Holy Spirit.

When Simon saw that the Holy Spirit was given when John and I placed our hands upon people's heads, he offered money to buy this power. "Let me have this power, too," he exclaimed, "so that when I lay my hands on people, they will receive the Holy Spirit!"

But I replied, "May your money perish with you for thinking God's gift can be bought! You can have no part in this, for your heart is not right before God. Turn from your wickedness and pray to the Lord. Perhaps he will forgive your evil thoughts, for I can see that you are full of bitterness and held captive by sin."

"Pray to the Lord for me," Simon exclaimed, "that these terrible things will not happen to me!"

After testifying and preaching the word of the Lord in Samaria, John and I returned to Jerusalem. And we stopped in many Samaritan villages along the way to preach the Good News to them, too.

Philip Baptized an Ethiopian

Chapter 8:26-40

As for Philip, an angel of the Lord said to him, "Go south down the desert road that runs from Jerusalem to Gaza." So he did, and he met the treasurer of Ethiopia, a eunuch of great authority under the queen of Ethiopia. The eunuch had gone to Jerusalem to worship, and he was now returning. Seated in his carriage, he was reading aloud from the book of the prophet Isaiah.

The Holy Spirit said to Philip, "Go over and walk along beside the carriage."

Philip ran over and heard the man reading from the prophet Isaiah; so he asked, "Do you understand what you are reading?"

The man replied, "How can I, when there is no one to instruct me?" And he begged Philip to come up into the carriage and sit with him. The passage of Scripture he had been reading was this:

> *He was led as a sheep to the slaughter. And as a lamb is silent before the shearers, he did not open his mouth. He was humiliated and received no justice. Who can speak of his descendants? For his life was taken from the earth.*
>
> Is. 53:7-8

The eunuch asked Philip, "Was Isaiah talking about himself or someone else?" So Philip began with this same Scripture and then used many others to tell him the Good News about Jesus.

As they rode along, they came to some water, and the eunuch said, "Look! There is some water! Why can I not be baptized?"

"You can," Philip answered, "if you believe with all your heart."

And the eunuch replied, "I believe that Jesus Christ is the Son of God."

And the eunuch ordered the carriage to stop, and they went down into the water, and Philip baptized him.

When they came up out of the water, the Spirit of the Lord caught Philip away. The eunuch never saw him again but went on his way rejoicing. Meanwhile, Philip found himself farther north at the city of Azotus! He preached the Good News there and in every city along the way until he came to Caesarea.

Saul Encounters Christ

Chapter 9:1-25

Meanwhile, Saul was uttering threats with every breath. He was eager to destroy the Lord's followers, so he went to the high priest. He requested letters addressed to the synagogues in Damascus, asking their cooperation in the arrest of any followers of the Way he found there. He wanted to bring them—both men and women—back to Jerusalem in chains.

Damascus, AD 37

As he was nearing Damascus on the mission, a brilliant light from heaven suddenly beamed down upon him! He fell to the ground and heard a voice saying to him, "Saul, Saul! Why are you persecuting me?"

"Who are you, sir?" Saul asked.

And the voice replied, "I am Jesus, the one you are persecuting! Now get up and go into the city, and you will be told what you are to do."

The men with Saul stood speechless with surprise, for they heard the sound of someone's voice, but they saw no one! As Saul picked himself up off the ground, he found that he was blind. So his companions led him by the hand to Damascus. He remained there blind for three days. And all that time he went without food and water.

Now there was a believer in Damascus named Ananias. The Lord spoke to him in a vision, calling, "Ananias!"

"Yes, Lord!" he replied.

The Lord said, "Go over to Straight Street, to the house of Judas. When you arrive, ask for Saul of Tarsus. He is praying to me right now. I have shown him a vision of a man named Ananias coming in and laying his hands on him so that he can see again."

"But Lord," exclaimed Ananias, "I have heard about the terrible things this man has done to the believers in Jerusalem! And we hear that he is authorized by the leading priests to arrest every believer in Damascus."

But the Lord said, "Go and do what I say. For Saul is my chosen instrument to take my message to the Gentiles and to kings, as well as to the people of Israel. And I will show him how much he must suffer for me."

So Ananias went and found Saul. He laid his hands on him and said, "Brother Saul, the Lord Jesus, who appeared to you on the road, has sent me so that you may get your sight back and be filled with the Holy Spirit." Instantly something like scales fell from Saul's eyes, and he regained his sight. Then he got up and was baptized. Afterward he ate some food and was strengthened.

Saul stayed with the believers in Damascus for a few days. And immediately he began preaching about Jesus in the synagogues, saying, "He is indeed the Son of God!"

All who heard him were amazed. "Is not this the same man who persecuted Jesus' followers with such devastation in Jerusalem?" they asked. "And we understand that he came here to arrest them and take them in chains to the leading priests."

Saul's preaching became more and more powerful, and the Jews in Damascus could not refute his proofs that Jesus was indeed the Messiah. After a while the Jewish leaders decided to kill him. But Saul was told about their plot, and that they were watching for him day and night at the city gate so they could murder him. So during the night, some of the other believers let him down in a large basket through an opening in the city wall.

I Met Saul for the First Time

Jerusalem, AD 40   Chapter 9:26-30

When Saul arrived in Jerusalem, he tried to meet with the believers, but they were all afraid of him. They thought he was only pretending to be a believer! Then Barnabas brought him to us apostles and told us what the Lord had said to Saul and how he boldly preached in the name of Jesus in Damascus. Then the other apostles and I accepted Saul, and after that he was constantly with us in Jerusalem, preaching boldly in the name of the Lord. He debated with some Greek-speaking Jews, but they plotted to murder him. When we believers heard about it, however, we took him to Caesarea and sent him on to his hometown of Tarsus.

I Healed a Man in Lydda

Chapter 9:31-38

The church then had peace throughout Judea, Galilee, and Samaria, and it grew in strength and numbers. We believers were walking in the fear of the Lord and in the comfort of the Holy Spirit.

I traveled from place to place to visit the other believers, and in my travels I came to the Lord's people in the town of Lydda. There I met a man named Aeneas, who had been paralyzed and bedridden for eight years. I said to him, "Aeneas, Jesus Christ heals you! Get up and make your bed!" And he was healed instantly. Then the whole population of Lydda and Sharon turned to the Lord when they saw Aeneas walking around.

There was a believer in Joppa named Tabitha (which in Greek is Dorcas). She was always doing kind things for others and helping the poor. About this time she became ill and died. Her friends prepared her for burial and laid her in an upstairs room. But they had heard that I was nearby at Lydda, so they sent two men to beg me, "Please come as soon as possible!"

I Healed a Woman in Joppa

So I returned with them; and as soon as I arrived, they took me to the upstairs room. The room was filled with widows who were weeping and showing me the coats and other garments Tabitha had made for them. But I asked them all to leave the room; then I knelt and prayed. Turning to the body I said, "Get up, Tabitha." And she opened her eyes! When she saw me, she sat up! I gave her my hand and helped her up. Then I called in the widows and all the believers, and I showed them that she was alive.

The news raced through the whole town, and many believed in the Lord. And I stayed a long time in Joppa, living with Simon, a leatherworker.

My Vision in Joppa

AD 41

In Caesarea there lived a Roman army officer named Cornelius, who was a captain of the Italian Regiment. He was a devout man who feared the God of Israel, as did his entire household. He gave generously to charity and was a man who regularly prayed to God. One afternoon about three o'clock, he had a vision in which he saw an angel of God coming toward him. "Cornelius," the angel said.

Cornelius stared at him in terror. "What is it, sir?" he asked the angel.

And the angel replied, "Your prayers and gifts to the poor have not gone unnoticed by God! Now send some men down to Joppa to find a man named Simon Peter. He is staying with Simon, a leatherworker who lives near the shore. Ask him to come and visit you."

As soon as the angel was gone, Cornelius called two of his household servants and a devout soldier, one of his personal attendants. He told them what had happened and sent them off to Joppa.

The next day as Cornelius's messengers were nearing the city, I went up to the flat roof to pray. It was about noon, and I was hungry. But while lunch was being prepared, I fell into a trance. I saw the sky open, and something like a large sheet was let down by its four corners. In the sheet were all sorts of animals, reptiles, and birds. Then a voice said to me, "Get up, Peter, kill and eat them."

"Never, Lord," I declared. "I have never in all my life eaten anything forbidden by our Jewish laws."

The voice spoke again, "If God says something is acceptable, do not say it isn't."

The same vision was repeated three times. Then the sheet was pulled up again to heaven.

I was very perplexed. What could the vision mean? Just then the men sent by Cornelius found the house and stood inside the gate. They asked if this was the place where I was staying. Meanwhile, as I was puzzling over the vision, the Holy Spirit said to me, "Three men have come looking for you. Go down and go with them without hesitation. All is well, for I have sent them."

So I went down and said, "I am the man you are looking for. Why have you come?"

They said, "We were sent by Cornelius, a Roman officer. He is a devout man who fears the God of Israel and is well respected by all the Jews. A holy angel instructed him to send for you so you can go to his house and give him a message."

So I invited the men to be my guests for the night. The next day I went with them, accompanied by some other believers from Joppa.

I Preached Christ to the Gentiles

We arrived in Caesarea the following day. Cornelius
was waiting for me and had called together his relatives and
close friends to meet me. As I entered his home, Cornelius
fell to the floor before me in worship. But I pulled him up
and said, "Stand up! I am a human being like you!" So
Cornelius got up, and we talked together and went inside
where the others were assembled.

I told them, "You know it is against the Jewish laws for
me to come into a Gentile home like this. But God has
shown me that I should never think of anyone as impure.
So I came as soon as I was sent for. Now tell me why you
sent for me."

Cornelius replied, "Four days ago I was praying in my
house at three o'clock in the afternoon. Suddenly, a man in
dazzling clothes was standing in front of me. He told me,
'Cornelius, your prayers have been heard, and your gifts to
the poor have been noticed by God! Now send some men
to Joppa and summon Simon Peter. He is staying in the
home of Simon, a leatherworker who lives near the shore.'
So I sent for you at once, and it was good of you to come.
Now here we are, waiting before God to hear the message
the Lord has given you."

Then I replied, "I see very clearly that God does not
show partiality. In every nation he accepts those who fear
him and do what is right. I am sure you have heard the
Good News for the people of Israel—that there is peace with
God through Jesus Christ, who is Lord of all. You know
what happened all through Judea, beginning in Galilee after
John the Baptist began preaching. And no doubt you know
that God anointed Jesus of Nazareth with the Holy Spirit
and with power. Then Jesus went around doing good and
healing all who were oppressed by the devil, for God was
with him.

"And we apostles are witnesses of all he did throughout
Israel and in Jerusalem. They put him to death by crucifying

him, but God raised him to life three days later. Then God allowed him to appear, not to the general public, but to us whom God had chosen beforehand to be his witnesses. We were those who ate and drank with him after he rose from the dead. And he ordered us to preach everywhere and to testify that Jesus is ordained of God to be the judge of all— the living and dead. He is the one all the prophets testified about, saying that everyone who believes in him will have their sins forgiven through his name."

Even as I was saying these things, the Holy Spirit fell upon all who had heard the message. The Jewish believers who came with me were amazed that the gift of the Holy Spirit had been poured out upon the Gentiles, too. And there could be no doubt about it, for they heard them speaking in tongues and praising God.

I Reported to the Other Eleven Apostles

Jerusalem   Chapter 11:1-18

Soon the news reached the apostles and believers in Judea that the Gentiles had received the word of God. But when I arrived back in Jerusalem, some of the Jewish believers criticized me. "You entered the home of Gentiles and even ate with them!"

Then I told them exactly what had happened. "One day in Joppa," I said, "while I was praying, I went into a trance and saw a vision. Something like a large sheet was let down by its four corners from the sky. And it came right down to me. When I looked inside the sheet, I saw all sorts of small animals, wild animals, reptiles, and birds that we are not allowed to eat. And I heard a voice say, 'Get up, Peter; kill and eat them.'

" 'Never, Lord,' I replied. 'I have never eaten anything forbidden by our Jewish laws.'

"But the voice from heaven came again, 'If God says something is acceptable, do not say it isn't.'

"This happened three times before the sheet and all it contained was pulled back up into heaven. Just then three

31

men who had been sent from Caesarea arrived at the house where I was staying. The Holy Spirit told me to go with them and not to worry about their being Gentiles. These six brothers here accompanied me, and we soon arrived at the home of the man who had sent for us. He told us how an angel had appeared to him in his home and had told him, 'Send messengers to Joppa to find Simon Peter. He will tell you how you and all you household will be saved!'

"Well, I began telling them the Good News, but just as I was getting started, the Holy Spirit fell on them, just as he fell on us at the beginning. Then I thought of the Lord's words when he said, 'John baptized with water, but you will be baptized with the Holy Spirit.' And since God gave these Gentiles the same gift he gave us when we believed in the Lord Jesus Christ, who was I to argue?"

When the others heard this, all their objections were answered and they began praising God. They said, "God has also given the Gentiles the privilege of turning from sin and receiving eternal life."

The Gospel and the Church Spread as Far as Antioch

Chapter 11:19-24

Meanwhile, the believers who had fled from Jerusalem during the persecution after Stephen's death traveled as far as Phoenicia, Cyprus, and Antioch of Syria. They preached the Good News, but only to Jews. However, some of the believers who went to Antioch from Cyprus and Cyrene began preaching to Gentiles about the Lord Jesus. The power of the Lord was upon them, and large numbers of these Gentiles believed and turned to the Lord.

When the church at Jerusalem heard what had happened, they sent Barnabas to Antioch. When he arrived and saw proof of God's favor, he was filled with joy, and he encouraged the believers to stay true to the Lord. Barnabas was a good man, full of the Holy Spirit and strong in faith. And large numbers of people were brought to the Lord.

BARNABAS

CONTINUES THE STORY

AD 41-44

Acts 11:25-30

I, Barnabas, Am Sent to Antioch

I, Barnabas, went on to Tarsus to find Saul. When I found him, I brought him back to Antioch. Both of us stayed there with the church for a full year, teaching great numbers of people. (It was there at Antioch that the believers were first called Christians.)

During this time, some prophets traveled from Jerusalem to Antioch. One of them named Agabus stood up in one of the meetings to predict by the Spirit that a great famine was coming upon the entire Roman world. (This was fulfilled during the reign of Claudius.) So the believers in Antioch decided to send relief to the brothers and sisters in Judea, everyone giving as much as they could. This they did, entrusting their gifts to Saul and me to take to the elders of the church in Jerusalem.

PETER

TAKES UP THE STORY AGAIN

AD 44

Acts 12:1-25

Herod Ordered My Imprisonment and James's Execution

About that time King Herod Agrippa began to persecute some believers in the church. He had the apostle James (John's brother) killed with a sword. When Herod saw how much this pleased the Jewish leaders, he arrested me, *Peter*, during the Passover celebration and imprisoned me, placing me under the guard of four squads of four soldiers each. Herod's intention was to bring me out for public trial after the Passover. But while I was in prison, the church prayed very earnestly for me.

The Angel of the Lord Set Me Free

The night before I was to be placed on trial, I was asleep, chained between two soldiers, with others standing guard at the prison gate. Suddenly, there was a bright light in the cell, and an angel of the Lord stood before me. The angel tapped me on the side to awaken me and said, "Quick! Get up!" And the chains fell off my wrists. Then the angel told me, "Get dressed and put on your sandals." And I did. "Now put on your coat and follow me," the angel ordered.

So I left the cell, following the angel. But all the time I thought it was a vision. I did not realize it was really happening. We passed the first and the second guard posts and came to the iron gate to the street, and this opened to us all by itself. So we passed through and started walking down the street, and then the angel suddenly left me.

I finally realized what had happened. "It's really true!" I said to myself. "The Lord has sent his angel and saved me from Herod and from what the Jews were hoping to do to me!"

After a little thought, I went to the home of Mary, the mother of John Mark, where many were gathered for prayer.

I knocked at the door in the gate, and a servant girl named Rhoda came to open it. When she recognized my voice, she was so overjoyed that, instead of opening the door, she ran back inside and told everyone, "Peter is standing at the door!"

"You are out of you mind," they said. When she insisted, they decided, "It must be his angel."

Meanwhile, I continued knocking. When they finally went out and opened the door, they were amazed. I motioned for them to quiet down and told them what had happened and how the Lord had led me out of jail. "Tell James and the other brothers what happened," I said. And then I went to another place.

At dawn, there was a great commotion among the soldiers about what had happened to me. Herod Agrippa ordered a thorough search for me. When I could not be found, Herod interrogated the guards and sentenced them to death. Afterward Herod left Judea to stay in Caesarea for a while.

Herod Was Struck Dead

Caesarea   Chapter 12:20-25

Now Herod was very angry with the people of Tyre and Sidon. So they sent a delegation to make peace with him because their cities were dependent upon Herod's country for their food. They made friends with Blastus, Herod's personal assistant, and an appointment with Herod was granted. When the day arrived, Herod put on his royal robes, sat on his throne, and made a speech to them. The people gave him a great ovation, shouting, "It is the voice of a god, not of a man!"

Instantly, an angel of the Lord struck Herod with a sickness, because he accepted the people's worship instead of giving glory to God. So he was consumed with worms and died.

But God's Good News was spreading rapidly, and there were many new believers.

BARNABAS

CONTINUES THE STORY

AD 47-50

Acts 13:1-15:35

Paul Is Sent to the Gentiles

Antioch, AD 47

Chapter 13:1-3

When Saul and I had finished our mission in Jerusalem, we returned to Antioch, taking John Mark with us.

Among the prophets and teachers of the church at Antioch of Syria were Simeon (called "the black man"), Lucius (from Cyrene), Manaen (the childhood companion of King Herod Antipas), Saul, and I, Barnabas. One day as we were worshiping the Lord and fasting, the Holy Spirit said, "Dedicate Barnabas and Saul for the special work I have for them." So after more fasting and prayer, the men laid their hands on us and sent us on our way.

Paul and I Journeyed to Cyprus and Galatia

AD 47

Chapter 13:4-51

Sent out by the Holy Spirit, Saul and I went down to the seaport of Seleucia and then sailed for the island of Cyprus. There in the town of Salamis, we went to the Jewish synagogues and preached the word of God. (John Mark went with us as our assistant.)

Afterward we preached from town to town across the entire island until finally we reached Paphos, where we met a Jewish sorcerer, a false prophet named Bar-Jesus. He had attached himself to the governor, Sergius Paulus, a man of considerable insight and understanding. The governor invited Saul and me to visit him, for he wanted to hear the word of God. But Elymas, the sorcerer (as his name means in Greek), interfered and urged the governor to pay no attention to what Saul and I said. He was trying to turn the governor away from the Christian faith.

Then Saul, also known as Paul, filled with the Holy Spirit, looked the sorcerer in the eye and said, "You son of the devil, full of every sort of trickery and villainy, enemy of all that is good, will you never stop perverting the true ways of the Lord? And now the Lord has laid his hand of punishment upon you, and you will be stricken awhile with blindness." Instantly mist and darkness fell upon him, and he began wandering around begging for someone to take his hand and lead him. When the governor saw what had happened, he believed and was astonished at what he learned about the Lord.

Now Paul and those of us with him left Paphos by ship for Pamphylia, landing at the port town of Perga. There John Mark left us and returned to Jerusalem. But Paul and I traveled inland to Antioch of Pisidia.

On the Sabbath we went to the synagogue for the services. After the usual readings from the books of Moses and from the Prophets, those in charge of the service sent us this message: "Brothers, if you have any word of encouragement for us, come and give it!"

So Paul stood, lifted his hand to quiet them, and started speaking. "People of Israel," he said, "and you devout Gentiles who fear the God of Israel, listen to me.

"The God of this nation of Israel chose our ancestors and made them prosper in Egypt. Then he powerfully led them out of their slavery. He put up with them through forty years of wandering around in the wilderness. Then he destroyed seven nations in Canaan and gave their land to Israel as an inheritance. All this took about 450 years. After that, judges ruled until the time of Samuel the prophet. Then the people begged for a king, and God gave them Saul of Kish, a man of the tribe of Benjamin, who reigned for forty years. But God removed him from the kingship and replaced him with David, a man about whom God said,

> *David son of Jesse is a man after my own heart, for he will do everything I want him to.*
>
> 1Sam. 13:14

"And it is one of King David's descendants, Jesus, who is God's promised Savior of Israel! But before Jesus came, John the Baptist preached the need for everyone in Israel to turn from sin and turn to God and be baptized. As John was finishing his ministry he asked,

Do you think I am the Messiah? No! But he is coming soon . . .and I am not even worthy to be his slave.

John 1:27

"Brothers—you sons of Abraham, and also all of you devout Gentiles who fear The God of Israel—this salvation is for us! The people in Jerusalem and their leaders fulfilled prophecy by condemning Jesus to death. They did not recognize him or realize that he is the one the prophets had written about, though they hear the prophets' words read every Sabbath. They found no just cause to execute him, but they asked Pilate to have him killed anyway.

"When they had fulfilled all the prophecies concerning his death, they took him down from the cross and placed him in a tomb. But God raised him from the dead! And he appeared over a period of many days to those who had gone with him from Galilee to Jerusalem—these are his witnesses to the people of Israel.

"And now Barnabas and I are here to bring you this Good News. God's promise to our ancestors has come true in our own time, in that God raised Jesus. This is what the second psalm is talking about when it says concerning Jesus,

You are my Son. Today I have become your Father.

Ps. 2:7

For God had promised to raise him from the dead, never again to die. This is stated in the Scripture that says,

I will give you the sacred blessings I promised to David.

Is. 55:3

Another psalm explains more fully, saying,

You will not allow your Holy One to rot in the grave.

Ps. 16:10

Now this is not a reference to David, for after David had served his generation according to the will of God, he died and was buried, and his body decayed. No, it was a reference to someone else—someone whom God raised and whose body did not decay.

"Brothers, listen! In this man Jesus there is forgiveness for your sins. Everyone who believes in him is freed from all guilt and declared right with God—something the Jewish law could never do. Be careful! Do not let the prophets' words apply to you. For they said,

> *Look, you mockers, be amazed and die! For*
> *I am doing something in your own day,*
> *something you would not believe even if*
> *someone told you about it."*
>
> Hab. 1:5

As Paul and I left the synagogue that day, the people asked us to return again and speak about these things the next week. Many Jews and godly converts to Judaism who worshiped at the synagogue followed Paul and me, and the two of us urged them, "By God's grace, remain faithful."

The following week almost the entire city turned out to hear us preach the word of the Lord. But when the Jewish leaders saw the crowds, they were jealous; so they slandered Paul and argued against whatever he said.

Then Paul and I spoke out boldly and declared, "It was necessary that this Good News from God be given first to you Jews. But since you have rejected it and judged yourselves unworthy of eternal life—well, we will offer it to Gentiles. For this is as the Lord commanded us when he said,

> *I have made you a light to the Gentiles, to*
> *bring salvation to the farthest corners of the*
> *earth.*
>
> Is. 49:6

When the Gentiles heard this, they were very glad and thanked the Lord for his message; and all who were

46

appointed to eternal life became believers. So the Lord's message spread throughout that region.

Then the Jewish leaders stirred up both the influential religious women and the leaders of the city, and they incited a mob against Paul and me and ran us out of town. But we shook off the dust of our feet against them and went to the city of Iconium. And the believers were filled with joy and with the Holy Spirit.

Upon Leaving Pamphylia
Paul and I Went to Iconium, Lystra and Derbe

Early AD 48   Chapter 14:1-26

In Iconium, Paul and I went together to the synagogue and preached with such power that a great number of both Jews and Gentiles believed. But the Jews who spurned God's message stirred up distrust among the Gentiles against Paul and me, saying all sorts of evil things about us. We apostles stayed there a long time, preaching boldly about the grace of the Lord. The Lord proved our message was true by giving us power to do miraculous signs and wonders. But the people of the city were divided in their opinion about us. Some sided with the Jews, and some with us.

A mob of Gentiles and Jews, along with their leaders, decided to attack and stone us. When we learned of it, we fled for our lives. We went to the region of Lycaonia, to the cities of Lystra and Derbe and the surrounding area, and we preached the Good News there.

While we were at Lystra, Paul and I came upon a man with crippled feet. He had been that way from birth, so he had never walked. He was listening as Paul preached, and Paul noticed him and realized he had faith to be healed. So Paul called to him in a loud voice, "Stand up!" And the man jumped to his feet and started walking.

When the listening crowd saw what Paul had done, they shouted in their local dialect, "These men are gods in human bodies!" They decided that I was the Greek god Zeus and that Paul, because he was the chief speaker, was Hermes.

The temple of Zeus was located on the outskirts of the city. The priest of the temple and the crowd brought oxen and wreaths of flowers, and they prepared to sacrifice to us at the city gates.

But when Paul and I heard what was happening, we tore our clothing in dismay and ran out among the people, shouting, "Friends, why are you doing this? We are merely human beings like yourselves! We have come to bring you the Good News that you should turn from these worthless things to the living God, who made heaven and earth, the sea, and everything in them. In earlier days he permitted all nations their own ways, but he never left himself without a witness. There were always his reminders, such as sending you rain and good crops and giving you food and joyful hearts." But even so, Paul and I could scarcely restrain the people from sacrificing to us.

Now some Jews arrived from Antioch and Iconium and turned the crowds into a murderous mob. They stoned Paul and dragged him out of the city, apparently dead. But as the believers stood around him, he got up and went back into the city. The next day he left with me for Derbe.

Fall-Winter AD 48

After preaching the Good News in Derbe and making many disciples, Paul and I returned again to Lystra, Iconium, and Antioch of Pisidia, where we strengthened the believers. We encouraged them to continue in the faith, reminding them that they must enter into the Kingdom of God through many tribulations. Paul and I also appointed elders in every church and prayed for them with fasting, turning them over to the care of the Lord, in whom they had come to trust. Then we traveled back through Pisidia to Pamphylia. We preached again in Perga, then went on to Attalia.

Paul and I Ended Our Journey

Antioch, Mid-Summer AD 49 Chapter 14:27-28

Finally, we returned by ship to Antioch of Syria, where our journey had begun and where we had been committed to the grace of God for the work we had now completed. Upon arriving in Antioch, we called the church together and reported about our trip, telling all that God had done and how he had opened the door of faith to the Gentiles, too. And we stayed there with the believers in Antioch a long time!

Jewish Legalists Caused Us Problems in Antioch

Early AD 50   Chapter 15:1-3

While Paul and I were at Antioch of Syria, some men from Judea arrived and began to teach the Christians: "Unless you keep the ancient Jewish custom of circumcision taught by Moses, you cannot be saved." Paul and I, disagreeing with them, argued forcefully and at length. Finally, Paul and I were sent to Jerusalem, accompanied by some local believers, to talk to the apostles and elders about this question. The church sent us and the other delegates to Jerusalem, and we stopped along the way in Phoenicia and Samaria to visit the believers. We told them—much to everyone's joy—that the Gentiles, too, were being converted.

NOTE

The Jews who came from Jerusalem-the ones who were teaching circumcision to the church in Antioch- also returned to Jerusalem. That is, all but one.

There were at least one or two who went up to Galatia to try to convince the men in the Gentile churches in Galatia to be circumcised. When the Jews arrived in Galatia they caused much confusion in the four churches.

Paul and Barnabus did not know these men had gone to Galatia. Paul did not learn that these Jews had caused havoc among the Gentile Christians until he was about to leave on his second journey.

49

Paul and I Met with the Twelve Apostles

When we arrived in Jerusalem, Paul and I were welcomed by the whole church, including the apostles and elders. We reported on what God had been doing through our ministry. But then some of the men who had been Pharisees before their conversion stood up and declared that all Gentile converts must be circumcised and be required to follow the law of Moses.

So the apostles and the church elders got together to decide this question. At the meeting, after a long discussion, Peter stood and addressed us as follows: "Brothers, you all know that God chose me from among you some time ago to preach to the Gentiles so that they could hear the Good News and believe. God, who knows people's hearts, confirmed that he accepts Gentiles by giving them the Holy Spirit, just as he gave him to us. He made no distinction between us and them, for he also cleansed their hearts through faith. Why are you now questioning God's way by burdening the Gentile believers with a yoke that neither we nor our ancestors were able to bear? We believe that we are saved the same way, by the special favor of the Lord Jesus."

There was no further discussion, and everyone listened as Paul and I told about the miraculous signs and wonders God had done through us among the Gentiles.

When we had finished, James stood and said, "Brothers, listen to me. Peter has told you about the time God first visited the Gentiles to take from them a people for himself. And this conversion of Gentiles agrees with what the prophets predicted. For instance, it is written:

'Afterward I will return, and I will restore the fallen kingdom of David. From the ruins I will rebuild it, and I will restore it, so that the rest of humanity might find the Lord, including the Gentiles—all those I have called to be mine.' This is what the Lord

*says, he who made these things known long
ago.*

Amos 9:11-12

"And so my judgment is that we should stop troubling
the Gentiles who turn to God, except that we should write
to them and tell them to abstain from eating meat sacrificed
to idols, from sexual immorality, and from consuming blood
or eating the meat of strangled animals. For these laws of
Moses have been preached in Jewish synagogues in every
city on every Sabbath for many generations."

Accompanied by Silas and Judas (also called Barsabbas), Paul and I Returned to Antioch with a Letter

Chapter 15:22-35

Then the apostles and elders and the whole church in
Jerusalem chose delegates, and they sent them to Antioch
of Syria with Paul and me to report on this decision. The
men chosen were two of the church leaders—Judas (also
called Barsabbas) and Silas. This is the letter we took along
with us:

*This letter is from the apostles and elders, your broth-
ers in Jerusalem. It is written to the Gentile believers in
Antioch, Syria, and Cilicia. Greetings!*

*We understand that some men from here have
troubled you and upset you with their teaching, but they
had no such instructions from us. So it seemed good to
us, having agreed on our decision, to send you these rep-
resentatives, along with our beloved Barnabas and Paul,
who have risked their lives for the sake of our Lord
Jesus Christ. So we are sending Judas and Silas to tell
you what we have decided concerning your question.*

*For it seemed good to the Holy Spirit and to us to lay no
greater burden on you than these requirements: You must
abstain from eating food offered to idols, from consuming blood or eating the meat of strangled animals, and
from sexual immorality. If you do this, you will do
well. Farewell.*

51

We four messengers went at once to Antioch, where we called a general meeting of the Christians and delivered the letter. And there was great joy throughout the church that day as they read this encouraging message.

Then Judas and Silas, both being prophets, spoke extensively to the Christians, encouraging and strengthening their faith. They stayed for a while, and then Judas and Silas were sent back to Jerusalem, with the blessings of the Christians, to those who sent them.*

Paul and I stayed in Antioch to assist many others who were teaching and preaching the word of the Lord there.

---

*15:33 Some manucscripts add verse 34, *But Silas decided to stay there.*

SILAS

CONTINUES THE STORY

AD 50-54

Acts 15:36-18:18

Paul and Barnabas Parted Company

After some time Paul said to Barnabas, "Let's return to each city where we previously preached the word of the Lord, to see how the new believers are getting along." Barnabas agreed and wanted to take along John Mark. But Paul disagreed strongly, since John Mark had deserted them in Pamphylia and had not shared in their work. Their disagreement over this was so sharp that they separated. Barnabas took John Mark with him and sailed to Cyprus.

Paul chose me, Silas, and the believers sent us off, entrusting us to the Lord's grace.

NOTE

Paul Wrote a Letter to the Churches in Galatia

Summer, AD 50

Just as Paul was about to leave Antioch for Galatia he received word that some religious Judaizers from Jerusalem had gone to Galatia to make the Gentiles obey the Law of Moses and be circumcised. Failing at that, these men attacked Paul's reputation, accusing him of many things. Paul sat down and wrote a letter to the four Galation churches. This letter was the first Christian literature ever penned.

I, Silas, Joined Paul on His Second Journey

AD 50

Paul and I traveled throughout Syria and Cilicia to strengthen the churches there.

We went first to Derbe and then on to Lystra. There we met Timothy, a young disciple whose mother was a Jewish believer, but whose father was a Greek. Timothy was well thought of by the believers in Lystra and Iconium, so Paul wanted him to join us on our journey. In deference to the Jews of the area, he arranged for Timothy to be circumcised before we left, for everyone knew that his father was a Greek. Then we went from town to town, explaining the decision regarding the commandments that were to be obeyed, as decided by the apostles and elders in Jerusalem. So the churches were strengthened in their faith and grew daily in numbers.

Next Paul and I traveled through the area of Phrygia and Galatia, because the Holy Spirit had told us not to go into the province of Asia at that time. Then coming to the borders of Mysia, we headed for the province of Bythynia, but again the Spirit of Jesus did not let us go. So instead, we went on through Mysia to the city of Troas.

That night Paul had a vision. He saw a man from Macedonia in northern Greece, pleading with him, "Come over here and help us." So we decided to leave for Macedonia at once, for we could only conclude that God was calling us to preach the Good News there.

Paul and I Went to Philippi in Northern Greece

Late Summer, AD 50   Chapter 16:11-15

We boarded a boat at Troas and sailed straight across to the island of Samothrace, and the next day we landed at Neapolis. From there we reached Philippi, a major city of the district of Macedonia and a Roman colony; we stayed there several days.

On the Sabbath we went a little way outside the city to a riverbank, where we supposed that some people met for prayer, and we sat down to speak with some women who had come together. One of them was Lydia from Thyatira, a merchant of expensive purple cloth. She was a worshiper of God. As she listened to us, the Lord opened her heart, and she accepted what Paul was saying. She was baptized along with other members of her household, and she asked us to be her guests. "If you agree that I am faithful to the

Lord," she said, "come and stay at my home." And she urged us until we did.

Paul Cast Out an Evil Spirit

Fall, AD 50   Chapter 16:16-21

One day as we were going down to the place of prayer, we met a demon-possessed slave girl. She was a fortune-teller who earned a lot of money for her masters. She followed along behind us shouting, "These men are servants of the Most High God, and they have come to tell you how to be saved."

This went on day after day until Paul got so exasperated that he turned and spoke to the demon within her. "I command you in the name of Jesus Christ to come out of her," he said. And instantly it left her.

Her masters' hopes of wealth were now shattered, so they grabbed Paul and me and dragged us before the authorities at the marketplace. "The whole city is in an uproar because of these Jews!" they shouted. "They are teaching the people to do things that are against Roman customs."

Paul and I Were Imprisoned in Philippi

Late AD 50   Chapter 16:22-40

A mob quickly formed against Paul and me, and the city officials ordered us stripped and beaten with wooden rods. We were severely beaten, and then we were thrown into prison. The jailer was ordered to make sure we did not escape. So he took no chances but put us into the inner dungeon and clamped our feet in stocks.

Around midnight, Paul and I were praying and singing hymns to God, and the other prisoners were listening. Suddenly, there was a great earthquake, and the prison was shaken to its foundations. All the doors flew open, and the chains of every prisoner fell off! The jailer woke up to see the prison doors wide open. He assumed the prisoners had escaped, so he drew his sword to kill himself. But Paul shouted to him, "Do not do it! We are all here!"

Trembling with fear, the jailer called for lights and ran to the dungeon and fell down before Paul and me. He brought us out and asked, "Sirs, what must I do to be saved?"

We replied, "Believe on the Lord Jesus and you will be saved, along with your entire household." Then we shared the word of the Lord with him and all who lived in his household. That same hour the jailer washed our wounds, and he and everyone in his household were immediately baptized. Then he brought us into his house and set a meal before us. He and his entire household rejoiced because they all believed in God.

The next morning the city officials sent the police to tell the jailer, "Let those men go!" So the jailer told Paul, "You and Silas are free to leave. Go in peace."

But Paul replied, "They have publicly beaten us without trial and jailed us—and we are Roman citizens. So now they want us to leave secretly? Certainly not! Let them come themselves to release us!"

When the police made their report, the city officials were alarmed to learn that Paul and I were Roman citizens. They came to the jail and apologized to us. Then they brought us out and begged us to leave the city. Paul and I then returned to the home of Lydia, where we met with the believers and encouraged them once more before leaving town.

Paul and I Arrived in Thessalonica

Winter-Spring, AD 51   Chapter 17:1-9

Now Paul and I traveled through the towns of Amphipolis and Apollonia and came to Thessalonica, where there was a Jewish synagogue. As was Paul's custom, he went to the synagogue service, and for three Sabbaths in a row he interpreted the Scriptures to the people. He was explaining and proving the prophecies about the sufferings of the Messiah and his rising from the dead. He said, "This Jesus I am telling you about is the Messiah." Some who listened were persuaded and became converts, including a large number of godly Greek men and also many important women of the city.

But the Jewish leaders were jealous, so they gathered some worthless fellows from the streets to form a mob and start a riot. They attacked the home of Jason, searching for Paul and me so they could drag us out to the crowd. Not finding us there, they dragged out Jason and some of the other believers instead and took them before the city council. "Paul and Silas have turned the rest of the world upside down, and now they are here disturbing our city," they shouted. "And Jason has let them into his home. They are all guilty of treason against Caesar, for they profess allegiance to another king, Jesus."

The people of the city, as well as the city officials, were thrown into turmoil by these reports. But the officials released Jason and the other believers after they had posted bail. That very night the believers sent Paul and me to Berea.

Paul Went to Berea;
Timothy and I Remained at Thessalonica

Summer, AD 51   Chapter 17:10-15

When we arrived at Berea, we went to the synagogue. And the people of Berea were more open-minded than those in Thessalonica, and they listened eagerly to Paul's message. They searched the Scriptures day after day to check up on Paul and me, to see if we were really teaching the truth. As a result, many Jews believed, as did some of the prominent Greek women and many men.

But when some Jews in Thessalonica learned that Paul was preaching the word of God in Berea, they went there and stirred up trouble. The believers acted at once, sending Paul on to the coast, while Timothy and I remained behind. Those escorting Paul went with him to Athens; then they returned to Berea with a message for Timothy and me to hurry and join him.

Paul's Adventure in Athens

While Paul was waiting for us in Athens, he was deeply troubled by all the idols he saw everywhere in the city. He went to the synagogue to debate with the Jews and the God-fearing Gentiles, and he spoke daily in the public square to all who happened to be there.

He also had a debate with some of the Epicurean and Stoic philosophers. When he told them about Jesus and his resurrection, they said, "This babbler has picked up some strange ideas." Others said, "He is pushing some foreign religion."

Then they took him to the Council of Philosophers. "Come and tell us more about this new religion," they said. "You are saying some rather startling things, and we want to know what it is all about." (It should be explained that all the Athenians as well as the foreigners in Athens seemed to spend all their time discussing the latest ideas.)

So Paul, standing before the Council, addressed them as follows: "Men of Athens, I notice that you are very religious, for as I was walking along I saw your many altars. And one of them had this inscription on it: 'To an Unknown God.' You have been worshiping him without knowing who he is, and now I wish to tell you about him.

"He is the God who made the world and everything in it. Since he is Lord of heaven and earth, he does not live in man-made temples, and human hands cannot serve his needs—for he has no needs. He himself gives life and breath to everything, and he satisfies every need there is. From one man he created all the nations throughout the whole earth. He decided beforehand which should rise and fall, and he determined their boundaries.

"His purpose in all of this was that the nations should seek after God and perhaps feel their way toward him and find him—though he is not far from any one of us. For in him we live and move and exist. As one of your own poets says, 'We are his offspring.' And since this is true, we should not think of God as an idol designed by craftsmen from gold or silver or stone. God overlooked people's former ignorance about these things, but now he commands everyone everywhere to turn away from idols and turn to him. For he has set a day for judging the world with justice by the man he has appointed, and he proved to everyone who this is by raising him from the dead."

When they heard Paul speak of the resurrection of a person who had been dead, some laughed, but others said, "We want to hear more about this later." That ended Paul's discussion with them, but some joined him and became believers. Among them were Dionysius, a member of the Council, a woman named Damaris, and others.

Paul Arrived in Corinth

Then Paul left Athens and went to Corinth.

NOTE

Paul Wrote a Letter to the Church in Thessalonica

Late Fall, AD 51

Paul wrote a second letter. (The first letter was to the four churches in Galatia.) This second epistle of Paul's is I Thessalonians.

When Paul arrived in Corinth-in southern Greece- he received word about the situation in Thessalonica. The church in Thessalonica was experiencing social ostracism from the rest of the city. There were also some misunderstandings in the gathering about what happens to a believer when he dies. Hence, the first letter to the gathering in the city of Thessalonica is written from Corinth in southern Greece.

In Corinth Paul became acquainted with a Jew named Aquila, born in Pontus, who had recently arrived from Italy with his wife, Priscilla. They had been expelled from Italy as a result of Claudius Caesar's order to deport all Jews from Rome. Paul lived and worked with them, for they were tentmakers just as he was.

Each Sabbath found Paul at the synagogue, trying to convince the Jews and Greeks alike.

After that Timothy and I came down from Macedonia.

NOTE

Paul Wrote a Second Letter to the Church in Thessalonica

Early AD 52

A short time after Paul entered Corinth, both Silas and Timothy came down from northern Greece and gave Paul a first-hand report on the situation in the church in Thessalonica. It seemed that a number of brothers in Thessalonica were so sure Jesus was coming soon that they stopped working for a living. Others seemed to misunderstand a great deal of Paul's words when he was in Thessalonica, as well as misunderstanding some of his words in his first letter. For this reason Paul wrote to them again.

Paul spent his full time preaching and testifying to the Jews, telling them, "The Messiah you are looking for is Jesus." But when the Jews opposed him and insulted him, Paul shook the dust from his robe and said, "Your blood be upon your own heads—I am innocent. From now on I will go to the Gentiles."

After that he stayed with Titius Justus, a Gentile who worshiped God and lived next door to the synagogue. Crispus, the leader of the synagogue, and all his household believed in the Lord. Many others in Corinth also became believers and were baptized.

One night the Lord spoke to Paul in a vision and told him, "Do not be afraid! Speak out! Do not be silent! For I am with you, and no one will harm you because many people here in this city belong to me." So Paul stayed there for the next year and a half, teaching the word of God.

Paul Was Dragged before the Corinthian Court

Summer, AD 53   Chapter 18:12-18

But when Gallio became governor of Achaia, some Jews rose in concerted action against Paul and brought him before the governor for judgment. They accused Paul of "persuading people to worship God in ways that are contrary to the law." But just as Paul started to make his defense, Gallio turned to Paul's accusers and said, "Listen, you Jews, if this were a case involving some wrongdoing or a serious crime, I would be obliged to listen to you. But since it is merely a question of words and names and your Jewish laws, you take care of it. I refuse to judge such matters." And he drove them out of the courtroom. The mob had grabbed Sosthenes, the leader of the synagogue, and had beaten him right there in the courtroom. But Gallio paid no attention.

Paul stayed in Corinth for some time after that and then said good-bye to the brothers and sisters and sailed for the coast of Syria, taking Priscilla and Aquila with him. (Earlier, at Cenchrea, Paul had shaved his head according to Jewish custom, for he had taken a vow.)

TIMOTHY

CONTINUES THE STORY

AD 54-57

Acts 18:19-20:4

Paul, Silas and I -Timothy - Left Corinth
and Went to Ephesus

Fall-Winter, AD 53   Chapter 18:19-22a

When we arrived at the port of Ephesus, Paul left us behind. But while he was there, he went to the synagogue to debate with the Jews. They asked him to stay longer, but he declined. So he left, saying, "I will come back later, God willing." Then he set sail from Ephesus. The next stop was at the port of Caesarea.

Paul Visited the Church in Jerusalem,
thus Ending His Second Journey

Spring, AD 54   Chapter 18:22b

From there Paul went up and visited the church at Jerusalem and then went back to Antioch.

Paul Began His Third Journey

Chapter 18:23

After spending some time in Antioch, Paul went back to Galatia and Phrygia, visiting all the believers, encouraging them and helping them to grow in the Lord.

The Appearance of Apollos in Corinth

Chapter 18:24-28

Meanwhile, a Jew named Apollos, an eloquent speaker who knew the Scriptures well, had just arrived at Ephesus from Alexandria in Egypt. He had been taught the way of the Lord and talked to others with great enthusiasm and accuracy about Jesus. However, he knew only about John's baptism. When Priscilla and Aquila heard him preaching boldly in the synagogue, they took him aside and explained the way of God more accurately.

Apollos had been thinking about going to Achaia, and the brothers and sisters in Ephesus encouraged him in this. They wrote to the believers in Achaia, asking them to welcome him. When he arrived there, he proved to be of great benefit to those who, by God's grace, had believed. He refuted all the Jews with powerful arguments in public debate. Using the Scriptures, he explained to them, "The Messiah you are looking for is Jesus."

Paul Journeyed to Ephesus

Summer, AD 54   Chapter 19:1-7

While Apollos was in Corinth, Paul traveled through the interior provinces. Finally, he came to Ephesus, where he found several believers. "Did you receive the Holy Spirit when you believed?" he asked them.

"No," they replied, "we do not know what you mean. We have not even heard that there is a Holy Spirit."

"Then what baptism did you experience?" he asked.

And they replied, "The baptism of John."

Paul said, "John's baptism was to demonstrate a desire to turn from sin and turn to God. John himself told the people to believe in Jesus, the one John said would come later."

As soon as they heard this, they were baptized in the name of the Lord Jesus. Then when Paul laid his hands on them, the Holy Spirit came on them, and they began to speak in tongues and to prophesy. There were about twelve men in all.

Paul Remained in Ephesus for Three Years

AD 54-57   Chapter 19:8-22

Then Paul went to the synagogue and preached boldly for the next three months, arguing persuasively about the Kingdom of God. But some rejected his message and publicly spoke against the Way, so Paul left the synagogue and took the believers with him. Then he began preaching daily at the lecture hall of Tyrannus. This went on for the next two years, so that people throughout the province of Asia—both Jews and Greeks—heard the Lord's message.

God gave Paul the power to do unusual miracles, so that even when handkerchiefs or cloths that had touched his skin were placed on sick people, they were healed of their diseases, and any evil spirits within them came out.

A team of Jews who were traveling from town to town casting out evil spirits tried to use the name of the Lord Jesus. The incantation they used was this: "I command you by Jesus, whom Paul preaches, to come out!" Seven sons of Sceva, a leading priest, were doing this. But when they tried it on a man possessed by an evil spirit, the spirit replied, "I know Jesus, and I know Paul. But who are you?" And he leaped on them and attacked them with such violence that they fled from the house, naked and badly injured.

The story of what happened spread quickly all through Ephesus, to Jews and Greeks alike. A solemn fear descended on the city, and the name of the Lord Jesus was greatly honored. Many who became believers confessed their sinful practices. A number of them who had been practicing magic brought their incantation books and burned them at a public bonfire. The value of the books was several million dollars. So the message about the Lord spread widely and had a powerful effect.

Afterward Paul felt impelled by the Holy Spirit to go over to Macedonia and Achaia before returning to Jerusalem. "And after that," he said, "I must go on to Rome!"

He sent two assistants, Erastus and me, Timothy, on ahead to Macedonia while he stayed a while longer in the province of Asia.

NOTE

Paul Wrote a Letter to the Church in Corinth

Early Summer, AD 57

While in Ephesus, just before the uproar in Ephesus broke out, Paul wrote a letter to Corinth. The assembly in Corinth was dividing along four lines. Those who loved signs and wonders; they were "of" Peter. Those who loved oratory and Greek wisdom; they were "of" Apollos. Those who were "with" Paul, the founder of the assembly in Corinth. The last group was the "Jesus only" group.

Paul also had received a long list of questions from the brothers and sisters in Corinth. His letter dealt with both the problems and the questions. I Corinthians was Paul's fourth letter. He probably sent the letter by a man named Sosthenes who was from Corinth. Shortly thereafter Paul sent Titus to Corinth to see how the church received Paul's letter.

The Riot in Ephesus

Early Summer, AD 57   Chapter 19:23-41

About that time, serious trouble developed in Ephesus concerning the Way. It began with Demetrius, a silversmith who had a large business manufacturing silver shrines of the Greek goddess Artemis. He kept many craftsmen busy. He called the craftsmen together, along with others employed in related trades, and addressed them as follows:

"Gentlemen, you know that our wealth comes from this business. As you have seen and heard, this man Paul has persuaded many people that handmade gods are not gods at all. And this is happening not only here in Ephesus but throughout the entire province! Of course, I am not just talking about the loss of public respect for our business. I am also concerned that the temple of the great goddess

Artemis will lose its influence and that Artemis—this magnificent goddess worshiped throughout the province of Asia and all around the world—will be robbed of her prestige!"

At this their anger boiled, and they began shouting, "Great is Artemis of the Ephesians!" A crowd began to gather, and soon the city was filled with confusion. Everyone rushed to the amphitheater, dragging along Gaius and Aristarchus, who were Paul's traveling companions from Macedonia. Paul wanted to go in, but the believers would not let him. Some of the officials of the province, friends of Paul, also sent a message to him, begging him not to risk his life by entering the amphitheater.

Inside, the people were all shouting, some one thing and some another. Everything was in confusion. In fact, most of them did not even know why they were there. Alexander was thrust forward by some of the Jews, who encouraged him to explain the situation. He motioned for silence and tried to speak in defense. But when the crowd realized he was a Jew, they started shouting again and kept it up for two hours: "Great is Artemis of the Ephesians! Great is Artemis of the Ephesians!"

At last the mayor was able to quiet them down enough to speak. "Citizens of Ephesus," he said. "Everyone knows that Ephesus is the official guardian of the temple of the great Artemis, whose image fell down to us from heaven. Since this is an indisputable fact, you should not be disturbed, no matter what is said. Do not do anything rash. You have brought these men here, but they have stolen nothing from the temple and have not spoken against our goddess. If Demetrius and the craftsmen have a case against them, the courts are in session and the judges can take the case at once. Let them go through legal channels. And if there are complaints about other matters, they can be settled in a legal assembly. I am afraid we are in danger of being charged with rioting by the Roman government, since there is no cause for all this commotion. And if Rome demands an explanation, we will not know what to say." Then he dismissed them, and they dispersed.

Paul Left Ephesus and Traveled
throughout Greece

When it was all over, Paul sent for the believers and
encouraged them. Then he said good-bye and left for
Macedonia. Along the way, he encouraged the believers in
all the towns he passed through.

NOTE

Paul Wrote a Second Letter to the
Church in Corinth

Fall, AD 57

*Paul left Asia Minor and sailed northwest across the
Agaean Sea to Philippi in northern Greece (Macedonia).
There Paul found Titus who had just come from Corinth
to Philippi. Titus reported to Paul that the state of the
assembly in Corinth was good.*

Only three months had passed since Paul had written
I Corinthians.

*He now sat down and wrote a second letter to the
gathering in Corinth. In this letter Paul told of his
experience in Ephesus. Shortly after writing this letter,
Paul left Philippi and visited the church in Corinth.* II
Corinthians *was Paul's fifth letter.*

Then Paul traveled down to southern Greece, where he
stayed three months.

NOTE

Paul Wrote a Letter to the
Church Being Formed in Rome

AD 57

While in Corinth Paul wrote his sixth letter. He wrote it to a church which was just then in the process of being born-the chuch in Rome. The letter to the Romans *was penned less than three months after Paul wrote* II Corinthians. *The letter is addressed to about forty people meeting in Priscilla's home in Rome. Those assembling in Rome came together from all over the empire to begin this new assembly .*

Paul was peparing to sail back to Syria when he discovered a plot by some Jews against his life, so he decided to return to Macedonia.

Several of us were traveling with him. We were Sopater of Berea, the son of Pyrrhus; Aristarchus and Secundus, from Thessalonica; Gaius, from Derbe; Tychicus and Trophimus, who were from the province of Asia; and I, Timothy.

LUKE

ONCE MORE TAKES UP

THE STORY

AD 58-61

Acts 20:5-28:31

Paul Awakened Eutychus from the Sleep of Death

Spring, AD 58

Chapter 20:5-12

They went ahead and waited for Paul and me, Luke, at Troas. As soon as the Passover season ended, we boarded a ship at Philippi in Macedonia and five days later arrived in Troas, where we stayed a week.

On the first day of the week, we gathered to break bread. Paul was preaching; and since he was leaving the next day, he talked until midnight. The upstairs room where we met was lighted with many flickering lamps. As Paul spoke on and on, a young man named Eutychus, sitting on the windowsill, became very drowsy. Finally, he sank into a deep sleep and fell three stories to his death below. Paul went down, bent over him, and took him into his arms. "Do not worry," he said, "he is alive!" Then we all went back upstairs and ate the Lord's Supper together. And Paul continued talking to us until dawn; then he left. Meanwhile, the young man was taken home unhurt, and everyone was greatly relieved.

Paul Met with the Elders of the Ephesian Church for a Final Farewell

Chapter 20:13-38

Paul went by land to Assos, where he had arranged for us to join him, and we went on ahead by ship. He joined us there and we sailed together to Mitylene. The next day we passed the island of Kios. The following day, we crossed to the island of Samos. And a day later we arrived at Miletus.

Paul had decided against stopping at Ephesus this time because he did not want to spend further time in the province of Asia. He was hurrying to get to Jerusalem, if possible, for the Festival of Pentecost. But when we landed at Miletus, he sent a message to the elders of the church at Ephesus, asking them to come down to meet him.

When they arrived he declard, "You know that from the day I set foot in the province of Asia until now I have done the Lord's work humbly—yes, and with tears. I have endured the trials that came to me from the plots of the Jews. Yet I never shrank from telling the truth, either publicly or in your homes. I have had one message for Jews and Gentiles alike—the necessity of turning from sin and turning to God, and of faith in our Lord Jesus.

"And now I know that none of you to whom I have preached the Kingdom will ever see me again. Let me say plainly that I have been faithful. No one's damnation can be blamed on me, for I did not shrink from declaring all that God wants for you.

"And now beware! Be sure that you feed and shepherd God's flock—his church, purchased with his blood—among whom the Holy Spirit has appointed you as elders. I know full well that false teachers, like vicious wolves, will come in among you after I leave, not sparing the flock. Even some of you will distort the truth in order to draw a following. Watch out! Remember the three years I was with you—my constant watch and care over you night and day, and my many tears for you.

"And now I entrust you to God and the word of his grace—his message that is able to build you up and give you an inheritance with all those he has set apart for himself.

"I have never coveted anyone's money or fine clothing. You know that these hands of mine have worked to pay my own way, and I have even supplied the needs of those who were with me. And I have been a constant example of how you can help the poor by working hard. You should remember the words of the Lord Jesus:

It is more blessed to give than to receive."

Mt. 10:8; Mk. 10:21; Lk. 6:34-35, 18:22

When he had finished speaking, he knelt and prayed with them. They wept aloud as they embraced him in farewell, sad most of all because he had said that they should never see him again. Then they accompanied him down to the ship.

Paul Is Warned not to Go to Jerusalem

Chapter 21:1-14

After saying farewell to the Ephesian elders, we sailed straight to the island of Cos. The next day we reached Rhodes and then went to Patara. There we boarded a ship sailing for the Syrian province of Phoenicia. We sighted the island of Cypress, passed it on our left, and landed at the harbor of Tyre, in Syria, where the ship was to unload. We went ashore, found the local believers, and stayed with them a week. These disciples prophesied through the Holy Spirit that Paul should not go to Jerusalem. When we returned to the ship at the end of the week, the entire congregation, including wives and children, came down to the shore with us. There we knelt, prayed, and said our farewells. Then we went aboard, and they returned home.

The next stop after leaving Tyre was Ptolemais, where we greeted the brothers and sisters but stayed only one day. Then we went on to Caesarea and stayed at the home of Philip the Evangelist, one of the seven men who had been chosen to distribute food. He had four unmarried daughters who had the gift of prophecy.

During our stay of several days, a man named Agabus, who also had the gift of prophecy, arrived from Judea. When he visited us, he took Paul's belt and bound his own feet and hands with it. Then he said, "The Holy Spirit declares, 'So shall the owner of this belt be bound by the Jewish leaders in Jerusalem and turned over to the Romans.'" When we heard this, we who were traveling with him, as well as the local believers, begged Paul not to go on to Jerusalem.

But he said, "Why all this weeping? You are breaking my heart! For I am ready not only to be jailed at Jerusalem but also to die for the sake of the Lord Jesus."

When it was clear that we could not persuade him, we gave up and said, "The will of the Lord be done."

Paul Met with the Leaders of the
Jerusalem Church

Shortly afterward, we packed our things and left for Jerusalem. Some believers from Caesarea accompanied us, and they took us to the home of Mnason, a man originally from Cyprus and one of the early disciples. All the brothers and sisters in Jerusalem welcomed us cordially.

The next day Paul went in with us to meet with James, and all the elders of the Jerusalem church were present. After greetings were exchanged, Paul gave a detailed account of the things God had accomplished among the Gentiles through his ministry.

After hearing this, they praised God. But then they said, "You know, dear brother, how many thousands of Jews have also believed, and they all take the law of Moses very seriously. Our Jewish Christians here at Jerusalem have been told that you are teaching all the Jews living in the Gentile world to turn their backs on the laws of Moses. They say that you teach people not to circumcise their children or follow other Jewish customs. Now what can be done? For they will certainly hear that you have come.

"Here is our suggestion. We have four men here who have taken a vow and are preparing to shave their heads. Go with them to the Temple and join them in the purification ceremony, and pay for them to have their heads shaved. Then everyone will know that the rumors are all false and that you yourself observe the Jewish laws.

"As for the Gentile Christians, all we ask of them is what we already told them in a letter: They should not eat food offered to idols, nor consume blood, nor eat meat from strangled animals, and they should stay away from all sexual immorality."

So Paul agreed to their request, and the next day he went through the purification ritual with the men and went to the Temple. Then he publicly announced the date when their vows would end and sacrifices would be offered for each of them.

A Few Zealous Jews Incited a Riot against Paul

Early Summer, AD 58   Chapter 21:27-40

The seven days were almost ended when some Jews from the province of Asia saw Paul in the Temple and roused a mob against him. They grabbed him, yelling, "Men of Israel! Help! This is the man who teaches against our people and tells everybody to disobey the Jewish laws. He speaks against the Temple—and he even defiles it by bringing Gentiles in!" (For earlier that day they had seen him in the city with Trophimus, a Gentile from Ephesus, and they assumed Paul had taken him into the Temple.)

The whole population of the city was rocked by these accusations, and a great riot followed. Paul was dragged out of the Temple, and immediately the gates were closed behind him. As they were trying to kill him, word reached the commander of the Roman regiment that all Jerusalem was in an uproar. He immediately called out his soldiers and officers and ran down among the crowd. When the mob saw the commander and the troops coming, they stopped beating Paul. The commander arrested him and ordered him bound with two chains. Then he asked the crowd who he was and what he had done. Some shouted one thing and some another. He could not find out the truth in all the uproar and confusion, so he ordered Paul to be taken to the fortress. As they reached the stairs, the mob grew so violent the soldiers had to lift Paul to their shoulders to protect him. And the crowd followed behind shouting, "Kill him, kill him!"

As Paul was about to be taken inside, he said to the commander, "May I have a word with you?"

"Do you know Greek?" the commander asked, surprised. "Are you not the Egyptian who led a rebellion some time ago and took four thousand members of the Assassins out into the desert?"

81

"No," Paul replied. "I am a Jew from Tarsus in Cilicia, which is an important city. Please, let me talk to these people." The commander agreed, so Paul stood on the stairs and motioned to the people to be quiet. Soon a deep silence enveloped the crowd, and he addressed them in their own language, Aramaic.

Paul Testified to the Crowd in His Defense

Chapter 22:1-23

"Brothers and esteemed fathers," Paul said, "listen to me as I offer my defense." When they heard him speaking in their own language, the silence was even greater. "I am a Jew, born in Tarsus, a city in Cilicia, and I was brought up and educated here in Jerusalem under Gamaliel. At his feet I learned to follow our Jewish laws and customs very carefully. I became very zealous to honor God in everything I did, just as all of you are today. And I persecuted the followers of the Way, hounding some to death, binding and delivering both men and women to prison. The high priest and the whole council of leaders can testify that this is so. For I received the letters from them to our Jewish brothers in Damascus, authorizing me to bring the Christians from there to Jerusalem, in chains, to be punished.

"As I was on the road, nearing Damascus, about noon a very bright light from heaven suddenly shone around me. I fell to the ground and heard a voice saying to me, 'Saul, Saul, why are you persecuting me?'

"'Who are you, sir?' I asked. And he replied, 'I am Jesus of Nazareth, the one you are persecuting.' The people with me saw the light but did not hear the voice.

"I said, 'What shall I do, Lord?' And the Lord told me, 'Get up and go into Damascus, and there you will be told all that you are to do.'

"I was blinded by the intense light and had to be led into Damascus by my companions. A man named Ananias lived there. He was a godly man in his devotion to the law, and he was well thought of by all the Jews of Damascus. He

82

came to me and stood beside me and said, 'Brother Saul, receive your sight.' And that very hour I could see him!

"Then he told me, 'The God of our ancestors has chosen you to know his will and to see the Righteous One and hear him speak. You are to take his message everywhere, telling the whole world what you have seen and heard. And now, why delay? Get up and be baptized, and have your sins washed away, calling on the name of the Lord.'

"One day after I returned to Jerusalem, I was praying in the Temple, and I fell into a trance. I saw a vision of Jesus saying to me, 'Hurry! Leave Jerusalem, for the people here will not believe you when you give them your testimony about me.'

"'But Lord.' I argued, 'they certainly know that I imprisoned and beat those in every synagogue who believed on you. And when your witness Stephen was killed, I was standing there agreeing. I kept the coats they laid aside as they stoned him.'

"But the Lord said to me, 'Leave Jerusalem, for I will send you far away to the Gentiles!'"

The crowd listened until Paul came to that word; then with one voice they shouted, "Away with such a fellow! Kill him, kill him! He is not fit to live!" They yelled, threw off their coats, and tossed handfuls of dust into the air.

Paul Is Imprisoned in Jerusalem

AD 58   Chapter 22:24-23:11

The commander brought Paul inside and ordered him lashed with whips to make him confess his crime. He wanted to find out why the crowd had become so furious. As they tied Paul down to lash him, Paul said to the officer standing there, "Is it legal for you to whip a Roman citizen who has not even been tried?"

The officer went to the commander and asked, "What are you doing? This man is a Roman citizen!"

So the commander went over and asked Paul, "Tell me, are you a Roman citizen?"

"Yes, I certainly am," Paul replied.

"I am, too," the commander muttered, "and it cost me plenty!"

"But I am a citizen by birth!"

The soldiers who were about to interrogate Paul quickly withdrew when they heard he was a Roman citizen, and the commander was frightened because he had ordered him bound and whipped.

The next day the commander freed Paul from his chains and ordered the leading priests into session with the Jewish high council. He had Paul brought before them to try to find out what the trouble was all about.

Gazing intently at the high council, Paul began: "Brothers, I have always lived before God in all good conscience!"

Instantly Ananias the high priest commanded those close to Paul to slap him on the mouth. But Paul said to him, "God will slap you, you whitewashed wall! What kind of judge are you to break the law yourself by ordering me struck like that?"

Those standing near Paul said to him, "Is that the way you talk to God's high priest?"

"I am sorry, brothers, I did not realize he was the high priest," Paul replied, "for the Scriptures say,

Do not speak evil of anyone who rules over you."

Ex. 22:28

Paul realized that some members of the high council were Sadducees and some were Pharisees, so he shouted, "Brothers, I am a Pharisee, as were all my ancestors! And I am on trial because my hope is in the resurrection of the dead!"

This divided the council—the Pharisees against the Sadducees—for the Sadducees say there is no resurrection or angels or spirits, but the Pharisees believe in all these. So a great clamor arose. Some of the teachers of religious law who were Pharisees jumped up to argue that Paul was right. "We see nothing wrong with him," they shouted. "Perhaps a spirit or angel spoke to him." The shouting grew louder and louder, and men were tugging at Paul from both sides, pulling him this way and that. Finally, the commander, fearing they would tear him apart, ordered his soldiers to take him away from them and bring him back to the fortress.

That night the Lord appeared to Paul and said, "Be encouraged, Paul. Just as you have told the people about me here in Jerusalem, you must preach the Good News in Rome."

A Plot to Assassinate Paul Is Foiled

Chapter 23:12-32

The next morning a group of Jews got together and bound themselves with an oath to neither eat nor drink until they had killed Paul. There were more than forty of them. They went to the leading priests and other leaders and told them what they had done. "We have bound ourselves under oath neither to eat nor drink until we have killed Paul. You and the high council should tell the commander to bring Paul back to the council again," they requested. "Pretend you want to examine his case more fully. We will kill him on the way."

But Paul's nephew heard their plan and went to the fortress and told Paul. Paul called one of the officers and said, "Take this young man to the commander. He has something important to tell him."

So the officer did, explaining, "Paul, the prisoner, called me over and asked me to bring this young man to you because he has something to tell you."

The commander took him by the arm, led him aside, and asked, "What is it you want to tell me?"

Paul's nephew told him, "Some Jews are going to ask you to bring Paul before the Jewish high council tomorrow, pretending they want to get some more information. But do not do it! There are more than forty men hiding along the way ready to jump him and kill him. They have vowed not to eat or drink until they kill him. They are ready, expecting you to agree to their request."

"Do not let a soul know you told me this," the commander warned the young man as he sent him away.

Then the commander called two of his officers and ordered, "Get two hundred soldiers ready to leave for Caesarea at nine o'clock tonight. Also take two hundred spearmen and seventy horsemen. Provide horses for Paul to ride, and get him safely to governor Felix." Then he wrote this letter to the governor:

From Claudius Lysias, to his Excellency, Governor Felix. Greetings!

This man was seized by some Jews, and they were about to kill him when I arrived with the troops. When I learned that he was a Roman citizen, I removed him to safety. Then I took him to their high council to try to find out what he had done. I soon discovered it was something regarding their religious law—certainly nothing worthy of imprisonment or death. But when I was informed of a plot to kill him, I immediately sent him to you. I have told his accusers to bring their charges before you.

So that night, as ordered, the soldiers took Paul as far as Antipatris. They returned to the fortress the next morning, while the horsemen took him on to Caesarea.

Paul Is Held for Trial in Caesarea

Chapter 23:33-35

When they arrived in Caesarea, they presented Paul and the letter to Governor Felix. He read it and then asked Paul what province he was from. "Cilicia," Paul replied.

"I will hear your case myself when your accusers arrive," the governor told him. Then the governor ordered him kept in the prison at Herod's headquarters.

Paul before Felix

Five days later Ananias, the high priest, arrived with some of the Jewish leaders and the lawyer Tertullus, to press charges against Paul. When Paul was called in, Tertullus laid charges against Paul in the following address to the governor:

"Your Excellency, you have given peace to us Jews and have enacted reforms for us. And for all of this we are very grateful to you. But lest I bore you, kindly give me your attention for only a moment as I briefly outline our case against this man. For we have found him to be a troublemaker, a man who is constantly inciting the Jews throughout the world to riots and rebellions against the Roman government. He is a ringleader of the sect known as the Nazarenes. Moreover he was trying to defile the Temple when we arrested him. (We would have judged him by our law, but Lysias, the commander of the garrison, came and took him violently away from us, commanding his accusers to come before you.)* You can find out the truth of our accusations by examining him yourself."

Then the other Jews chimed in, declaring that everything Tertullus said was true.

Now it was Paul's turn. The governor motioned for him to rise and speak. Paul said, "I know, sir, that you have been a judge of Jewish affairs for many years, and this gives me confidence as I make my defense. You can quickly discover that it was no more than twelve days ago that I arrived in Jerusalem to worship at the Temple. I did not argue with anyone in the Temple, nor did I incite a riot in any synagogue or on the streets of the city. These men certainly cannot prove the things they accuse me of doing.

"But I admit that I follow the Way, which they call a sect. I worship the God of our ancestors, and I firmly believe the Jewish law and everything written in the books of prophecy. I have hope in God, just as these men do, that

---

Not all manuscripts include this verse.

87

he will raise both the righteous and the ungodly. Because of this, I always try to maintain a clear conscience before God and everyone else.

"After several years away, I returned to Jerusalem with money to aid my people and to offer sacrifices to God. My accusers saw me in the Temple as I was completing a purification ritual. There was no crowd around me and no rioting. But some Jews from the province of Asia were there—and they ought to be here to bring charges if they have anything against me! Ask these men here what wrongdoing the Jewish high council found in me, except for one thing I said when I shouted out, 'I am on trial before you today because I believe in the resurrection of the dead!'"

Felix, who was quite familiar with the Way, adjourned the hearing and said, "Wait until Lysias, the garrison commander, arrives. Then I will decide the case." He ordered an officer to keep Paul in custody but to give him some freedom and allow his friends to visit him and take care of his needs.

A few days later Felix came with his wife, Drusilla, who was Jewish. Sending for Paul, they listened as he told them about faith in Christ Jesus. As he reasoned with them about righteousness and self-control and the judgment to come, Felix was terrified. "Go away for now," he replied. "When it is more convenient, I will call you again." He also hoped that Paul would bribe him, so he sent for him quite often and talked with him.

Two years went by in this way; then Felix was succeeded by Porcius Festus. And because Felix wanted to gain favor with the Jewish leaders, he left Paul in prison.

Paul before Festus

Spring, AD 60

Chapter 25:1-12

Three days after Festus arrived in Caesarea to take over his new responsibilities, he left for Jerusalem, where the leading priests and other Jewish leaders met with him and made their accusations against Paul. They asked Festus as a favor to transfer Paul to Jerusalem. (Their plan was to waylay and kill him.) But Festus replied that Paul was at Caesarea and he himself would be returning there soon. So he said, "Those of you in authority can return with me. If Paul has done anything wrong, you can make your accusations."

Eight or ten days later he returned to Caesarea, and on the following day Paul's trial began. On Paul's arrival in court, the Jewish leaders from Jerusalem gathered around and made many serious accusations they could not prove. Paul denied the charges. "I am not guilty," he said. "I have committed no crime against the Jewish laws or the Temple or the Roman government."

Then Festus, wanting to please the Jews, asked him, "Are you willing to go to Jerusalem and stand trial before me there?"

But Paul replied, "No! This is the official Roman court, so I ought to be tried right here. You know very well I am not guilty. If I have done something worthy of death, I do not refuse to die. But if I am innocent, neither you nor anyone else has a right to turn me over to these men to kill me. I appeal to Caesar!"

Festus conferred with his advisers and then replied, "Very well! You have appealed to Caesar, and to Caesar you shall go!"

Paul before King Agrippa

Summer, AD 60   Chapter 25:13-26:32

A few days later King Agrippa arrived with his sister, Bernice, to pay their respects to Festus. During their stay of several days, Festus discussed Paul's case with the king. "There is a prisoner here," he told him, "whose case was left for me by Felix. When I was in Jerusalem, the leading priests and other Jewish leaders pressed charges against him and asked me to sentence him. Of course, I quickly pointed out to them that Roman law does not convict people without a trial. They are given an opportunity to defend themselves face to face with their accusers.

"When they came here for the trial, I called the case the very next day and ordered Paul brought in. But the accusations made against him were not at all what I expected. It was something about their religion and about someone called Jesus who died, but whom Paul insists is still alive. I was perplexed as to how to conduct an investigation of this kind, and I asked him whether he would be willing to stand trial on these charges in Jerusalem. But Paul appealed to the emperor. So I ordered him back to jail until I could arrange to send him to Caesar."

"I would like to hear the man myself," Agrippa said.

And Festus replied, "You shall—tomorrow!"

So the next day Agrippa and Bernice arrived at the auditorium with great pomp, accompanied by military officers and prominent men of the city. Festus ordered that Paul be brought in. Then Festus said, "King Agrippa and all present, this is the man whose death is demanded both by the local Jews and by those in Jerusalem. But in my opinion he has done nothing worthy of death. However, he appealed his case to the emperor, and I decided to send him. So I have brought him before all of you, and especially you, King Agrippa, so that after we examine him, I might have something to write. For it does not seem reasonable to send a prisoner to the emperor without specifying the charges against him!"

Then Agrippa said to Paul, "You may speak in your defense."

So Paul, with a gesture of his hand, started his defense: "I am fortunate, King Agrippa, that you are the one hearing my defense against all these accusations made by the Jewish leaders, for I know you are an expert on Jewish customs and controversies. Now please listen to me patiently!

"As the Jewish leaders are well aware, I was given a thorough Jewish training from my earliest childhood among my own people and in Jerusalem. If they would admit it, they know that I have been a member of the Pharisees, the strictest sect of our religion. Now I am on trial because I am looking forward to the fulfillment of God's promise made to our ancestors. In fact, that is why the twelve tribes of Israel worship God night and day, and they share the same hope I have. Yet, O king, they say it is wrong for me to have this hope! Why does it seem incredible to any of you that God can raise the dead?

"I used to believe that I ought to do everything I could to oppose the followers of Jesus of Nazareth. Authorized by the leading priests, I caused many of the believers in Jerusalem to be sent to prison. And I cast my vote against them when they were condemned to death. Many times I had them whipped in the synagogues to try to get them to curse Christ. I was so violently opposed to them that I even hounded them in distant cities of foreign lands.

"One day I was on such a mission to Damascus, armed with the authority and commission of the leading priests. About noon, Your Majesty, a light from heaven brighter than the sun shone down on me and my companions. We all fell down, and I heard a voice saying to me in Aramaic, 'Saul, Saul, why are you persecuting me? It is hard for you to fight against my will.'

"'Who are you, sir?' I asked.

"And the Lord replied, 'I am Jesus, the one you are persecuting. Now stand up! For I have appeared to you to appoint you as my servant and my witness. You are to tell the world about this experience and about other times I will appear to you. And I will protect you from both your own people and the Gentiles. Yes, I am going to send you to the Gentiles, to open their eyes so they may turn from darkness to light, and from the power of Satan to God. Then they will receive forgiveness for their sins and be given a place among God's people, who are set apart by faith in me.'

"And so, O King Agrippa, I was not disobedient to that vision from heaven. I preached first to those in Damascus, then in Jerusalem and throughout all Judea, and also to the Gentiles, that all must turn from their sins and turn to God—and prove they have changed by the good things they do. Some Jews arrested me in the Temple for preaching this, and they tried to kill me. But God protected me so that I am still alive today to tell these facts to everyone, from the least to the greatest. I teach nothing except what the prophets and Moses said would happen—that the Messiah would suffer and be the first risen from the dead as a light to Jews and Gentiles alike."

Suddenly Festus shouted, "Paul, you are insane. Too much study has made you crazy!"

But Paul replied, "I am not insane, Most Excellent Festus. I am speaking the sober truth. And King Agrippa knows about these things. I speak frankly, for I am sure these events are all familiar to him, for they were not done in a corner! King Agrippa, do you believe the prophets? I know you do—"

Agrippa interrupted him. "Do you think you can make me a Christian so quickly?"

Paul replied, "Whether quickly or not, I pray to God that both you and everyone here in this audience might become the same as I am, except for these chains."

Then the king, the governor, Bernice, and all the others stood and left. As they talked it over they agreed, "This man has not done anything worthy of death or imprisonment." And Agrippa said to Festus, "He could be set free if he had not appealed to Caesar!"

Paul Set Sail for Rome

AD 60   Chapter 27:1-9

When the time came, we set sail for Italy. Paul and several other prisoners were placed in the custody of an army officer named Julius, a captain of the Imperial Regiment. And Aristarchus, a Macedonian from Thessalonica, was also with us. We left on a boat whose home port was Adramyttium; it was scheduled to make several stops at ports along the coast of the province of Asia.

The next day when we docked at Sidon, Julius was very kind to Paul and let him go ashore to visit with friends so they could provide for his needs. Putting out to sea from there, we encountered headwinds that made it difficult to keep the ship on course, so we sailed north of Cyprus between the island and the mainland. We passed along the coast of the provinces of Cilicia and Pamphylia, landing at Myra, in the province of Lycia. There the officer found an

Egyptian ship from Alexandria that was bound for Italy, and he put us on board.

We had several days of rough sailing, and after great difficulty we finally neared Cnidus. But the wind was against us, so we sailed down to the leeward side of Crete, past the cape of Salmone. We struggled along the coast with great difficulty and finally arrived at Fair Havens, near the city of Lasea. We had lost a lot of time. The weather was becoming dangerous for long voyages by then because it was so late in the fall, and Paul spoke to the ship's officer about it.

The Shipwreck

Fall, AD 60   Chapter 27:10-44

"Sirs," he said, "I believe there is trouble ahead if we go on—shipwreck, loss of cargo, injuries, and danger to our lives." But the officer in charge of the prisoners listened more to the ship's captain and the owner than to Paul. And since Fair Havens was an exposed harbor—a poor place to spend the winter—most of the crew wanted to go to Phoenix, further up the coast of Crete, and spend the winter there. Phoenix was a good harbor with only a southwest and northwest exposure.

When a light wind began blowing from the south, the sailors thought they could make it. So they pulled up anchor and sailed along close to the shore. But the weather changed abruptly, and a wind of typhoon strength (a "northeaster," they called it) caught the ship and blew it out to sea. They could not turn the ship into the wind, so they gave up and let it run before the gale.

We sailed behind a small island named Cauda, where with great difficulty we hoisted aboard the lifeboat that was being towed behind us. Then we banded the ship with ropes to strengthen the hull. The sailors were afraid of being driven across the sandbars of Syrtis off the African coast, so they lowered the sea anchor and were thus driven before the wind.

93

The next day, as gale-force winds continued to batter the ship, the crew began throwing the cargo overboard. The following day they even threw out the ship's equipment and anything else they could lay their hands on. The terrible storm raged unabated for many days, blotting out the sun and the stars, until at last all hope was gone.

No one had eaten for a long time. Finally, Paul called the crew together and said, "Men, you should have listened to me in the first place and not left Fair Havens. You would have avoided all this injury and loss. But take courage! None of you will lose your lives, even though the ship will go down. For last night an angel of the God to whom I belong and whom I serve stood beside me, and he said, 'Do not be afraid, Paul, for you will surely stand trial before Caesar! What's more, God in his goodness has granted safety to everyone sailing with you.' So take courage! For I believe God. It will be just as he said. But we will be shipwrecked on an island."

About midnight on the fourteenth night of the storm, as we were being driven across the Sea of Adria, the sailors sensed land was near. They took soundings and found the water was only 120 feet deep. A little later they sounded again and found only 90 feet. At this rate they were afraid we would soon be driven against the rocks along the shore, so they threw out four anchors from the stern and prayed for daylight. Then the sailors tried to abandon the ship; they lowered the lifeboat as though they were going to put out anchors from the prow. But Paul said to the commanding officer and the soldiers, "You will all die unless the sailors stay aboard." So the soldiers cut the ropes and let the boat fall.

As the darkness gave way to the early morning light, Paul begged everyone to eat. "You have not touched food for two weeks," he said. "Please eat something now for your own good. For not a hair of your heads will perish." Then he took some bread, gave thanks to God before them all, and broke off a piece and ate it.

Then everyone was encouraged, and all 276 of us began to eat—for that is the number we had aboard. After eating, the crew lightened the ship further by throwing the cargo of wheat overboard.

When morning dawned, they did not recognize the coastline, but they saw a bay with a beach and wondered if they could get between the rocks and get the ship safely ashore. So they cut off the anchors and left them in the sea. Then they lowered the rudders, raised the foresail, and headed toward shore. But the ship hit a shoal and ran aground. The bow of the ship stuck fast, while the stern was repeatedly smashed by the force of the waves and began to break apart.

The soldiers wanted to kill the prisoners to make sure they did not swim ashore and escape. But the commanding officer wanted to spare Paul, so he did not let them carry out their plan. Then he ordered all who could swim to jump overboard first and make for land, and he told the others to try for it on planks and debris from the broken ship. So everyone escaped safely ashore!

We Were Marooned on the Island of Malta

November, AD 60 Chapter 28:1-10

Once we were safe on shore, we learned that we were on the island of Malta. The people of the island were very kind to us. It was cold and rainy, so they built a fire on the shore to welcome us and warm us.

As Paul gathered an armful of sticks and was laying them on the fire, a poisonous snake, driven out by the heat, fastened itself onto his hand. The people of the island saw it hanging there and said to each other, "A murderer, no doubt! Though he escaped the sea, justice will not permit him to live." But Paul shook off the snake into the fire and was unharmed. The people waited for him to swell up or suddenly drop dead. But when they had waited a long time and saw no harm come to him, they changed their minds and decided he was a god.

Near the shore where we had landed was an estate belonging to Publius, the chief official of the island. He welcomed us courteously and fed us for three days. As it happened, Publius's father was ill with fever and dysentery. Paul went in and prayed for him, and laying his hands on him, he healed him. Then all the other sick people on the island came and were cured. As a result we were showered with honors, and when the time came to sail, people put on board all sorts of things we would need for the trip.

We Continued toward Rome

February, AD 61   Acts 28:11-14

It was three months after the shipwreck that we set sail on another ship that had wintered at the island—an Alexandrian ship with the twin gods as its figurehead. Our first stop was Syracuse, where we stayed three days. From there we sailed across to Rhegium. A day later a south wind began blowing, so the following day we sailed up the coast of Puteoli. There we found some believers, who invited us to stay with them seven days. And so we came to Rome.

We Met the Believers from Rome

Spring, AD 61   Chapter 28:15-31

The brothers and sisters in Rome had heard we were coming, and they came to meet us at the Forum on the Appian Way. Others joined us at The Three Taverns. When Paul saw them, he thanked God and took courage.

When we arrived in Rome, Paul was permitted to have his own private lodging, though he was guarded by a soldier.

Three days after Paul's arrival, he called together the local Jewish leaders. He said to them, "Brothers, I was arrested in Jerusalem and handed over to the Roman governor, even though I had done nothing against our people or the customs of our ancestors. The Romans tried me and wanted to release me, for they found no cause for the death sentence. But when the Jewish leaders protested their decision, I felt it necessary to appeal to Caesar, even though

I had no desire to press charges against my own people. I asked you to come here today so we could get acquainted and so I could tell you that I am bound with this chain because I believe that the hope of Israel—the Messiah—has already come."

They replied, "We have heard nothing against you. We have had no letters from Judea or reports from anyone who has arrived here. But we want to hear what you believe, for the only thing we know about these Christians is that they are denounced everywhere."

So a time was set, and on that day a large number of people came to Paul's house. He told them about the Kingdom of God and taught them about Jesus from the Scriptures—from the five books of Moses and the books of the prophets. He began lecturing in the morning and went on into the evening. Some believed and some did not. But after they had argued back and forth among themselves, they left with this final word from Paul: "The Holy Spirit was right when he said to our ancestors through Isaiah the prophet,

> *Go and say to my people, 'You will hear my*
> *words, but you will not understand; you will*
> *see what I do, but you will not perceive its*
> *meaning.' For the hearts of these people are*
> *hardened, and their ears cannot hear, and*
> *they have closed their eyes—so their eyes*
> *cannot see, and their ears cannot hear, and*
> *their heart cannot understand, and they*
> *cannot turn to me and let me heal them.*
>
> Is. 6:9-10

So I want you to realize that this salvation from God is also available to the Gentiles, and they will accept it." And when he had said these words, the Jews departed, greatly disagreeing with each other.

For the next two years, Paul lived in his own rented house. He welcomed all who visited him, proclaiming the Kingdom of God with all boldness and teaching about the Lord Jesus Christ. And no one tried to stop him.

Spring AD 63

Luke's story of Acts ends in the Spring of AD 63.

A
LIST OF THE
LETTERS
WHICH PAUL WROTE
AFTER
THE CLOSE OF THE
BOOK OF ACTS

NOTE

While still in prison in Rome, Paul wrote a letter to the believers in Colossae in AD 61.

At the same time he wrote a circuit letter to the believers in Laodicea and Hierapolis.

(Some 300 years after this letter was written, unfortunately it came to be known as the letter to the Ephesians. Actually, it was written to the church in Colossae, Laodicea and Hierapolis. See Colossians 4:13-17.)

At this same time Paul also wrote to Philemon concerning Philemon's slave whose name was Onesimus.

Six months later (AD 61-62) Paul wrote a letter to the believers in Philippi.

After this, in AD 63, Paul wrote a letter to Timothy, and about the same time he wrote one to Titus.

Paul wrote his last known letter, to Timothy, in AD 66 or 67. This letter was written shortly before Paul's execution.

ೞಬಿಂೞಬಿಂ

Colossians	AD 61
Ephesians	AD 61
Philemon	AD 61
Philippians	AD 62
I Timothy	AD 63
Titus	AD 63
II Timothy	AD 67

CONTENTS

PETER BEGINS THE STORY, AD 30-41

BARNABAS CONTINUES THE STORY, AD 41-44

PETER TAKES UP THE STORY AGAIN, AD 44

BARNABAS CONTINUES THE STORY, AD 47-50

SILAS CONTINUES THEIR STORY, AD 50-54

The Book of Acts in First Person has a companion book. This book is called *The Story of My Life as Told by Jesus Christ*. It combines Matthew, Mark, Luke and John, blending them into one story. The book is writen in first person; that is, it reads as though Jesus Christ were telling his own story.

The life of Christ in frst person
Acts in first person

Published by
SEEDSOWERS
Christian Books Publishing House
P.O. BOX 3317
Jacksonville, FL 32206
(800) 228-2665
www.seedsowers.com